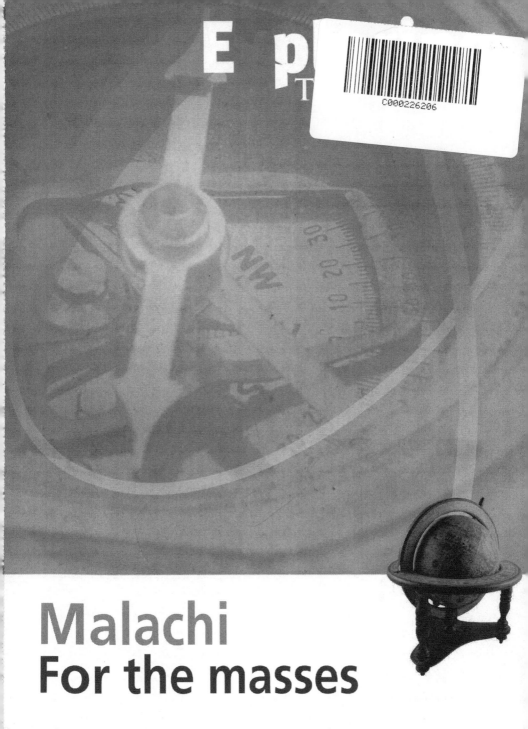

E p
T

Malachi
For the masses

Rich Castro

DayOne

© Day One Publications 2019

ISBN 978-1-84625-640-0
All Scripture quotations, unless stated otherwise, are from the anglicized edition of
the ESV Bible copyright © 2002 Collins, part of HarperCollins Publishers.

British Library Cataloguing in Publication Data available

Published by Day One Publications
Ryelands Road, Leominster, HR6 8NZ
Telephone 01568 613 740 FAX 01568 611 473
email—sales@dayone.co.uk
web site—www.dayone.co.uk
North America—email—usasales@dayone.co.uk

Cover design by Kathryn Chedgzoy
Printed by 4edge Limited

To my dear wife, Emma

This book is an excellent introduction to Malachi. It is not a technical commentary, but deals accessibly and succinctly with questions relating to the Hebrew when necessary. Castro writes well, handles Scripture carefully, and gets right to the heart of what these challenging passages have to say to God's people today.

Tony Watkins, speaker and writer on media and the Bible

Contents

Foreword

Malachi stands at a strategic place in history. As the final book in our Old Testament, it is the last written voice to Israel, and so stands as a gateway in the city walls awaiting the arrival of the King. Obviously it was written for the Jews of his day, and to miss this would be to present a dishonest exposition of the message. But, as Rich Castro shows, it has natural implications for the church of today, too. Malachi looks back to the earlier books of the Old Testament, but it is also fulfilled in the New Testament in the life of Christ's church. Moreover, as Malachi's original audience awaited the arrival of the king, so we wait at the gateway for the return of our King, and thus the author points us forward to Revelation.

Rich opens our eyes to this book in a powerful way. If you read the first chapter on the first five verses of Malachi, you will be eager to read on because it will warm your heart and lead you to come humbly before God and to praise him for who he is.

It is a book for Christians, yes, but it is also a book you can confidently pass on to non-believers. Rich has a powerful gospel message to share with his readers—as does the LORD through Malachi. I would love to share sections of this book to show you what a blessing it is, but I can only do that by taking them out of context, and that would rob you of their force!

You will be encouraged in reading this book, but you will also be challenged as a Christian. I found that I could not read it without both of those aspects coming to the fore. If that is not your experience, read it again!

Dr John Peet

Author, chemist and former travelling secretary for the Biblical Creation Society in the UK

Speaking in the storm

J ason left the station and crossed the park opposite. The rain was easing off, but he still had his coat collar turned up against the wet breeze. The night sky was especially dark, and the street lights fought to be seen through the drizzle. His shoes threatened to slide on the wet pavement, and he shivered slightly as he moved beyond the shelter of a large oak in the park's centre.

A streak of lightning and thunder directly overhead startled him, but in normal circumstances he would have continued his driving pace towards home without further thought. What actually happened was not only deeply shocking, but its effect was to stay with him for the rest of his life. It was as if time had stopped, as if someone had pressed the cosmic 'pause' button. Jason was no longer walking. He was stock still, rooted to the spot even as the rain fell around him. The preternatural light that broke through the clouds that night was brighter than lightning and fell in a steady glare. But it was the voice that made the greatest impression. It sounded deep, sonorous, resonating. The ground shook. The voice reverberated inside his head and made his ears tingle. His eyes blinked in the glare. His throat was impossibly dry and he could not swallow. And the voice—it was definitely a voice—became words: words which drove deep into his heart, pierced all his defences and laid him bare; words which he would never forget. The words of God. Jason stood statuesque.

If anyone needs a vivid encounter with the living God, it is you and I. Yet so commonly we forget that the Bible is as described above: God parting the clouds and addressing us directly. Recently, I overheard a conversation between two religious studies teachers. One of them was explaining that his standard punishment for misbehaviour in class was to get a student to copy out a chapter or two of Leviticus. Why? 'Because it's obscure and no one finds it interesting.' He did not realize that the Bible is God parting the clouds and addressing us. If he had known, he would have found Leviticus fascinating, challenging, encouraging, engaging, perhaps life-changing. Often we fail to realize this, too. We forget that the Bible is God's holy, inerrant, infallible and true word, deep, sonorous and resonating. This book is the Almighty Creator God speaking to us. We should not forget!

The word 'Malachi' literally means 'my messenger'. It is likely, too, that the name contains a shortened form of 'God', so that the word means more specifically, 'messenger of God'. There is considerable discussion in the commentaries about whether or not this is a designation or a proper noun, but in the light of the similarity between this prophetic introduction and the introduction to Isaiah and Zechariah (for example), it seems most likely that it is indeed a proper noun. In other words, as we may expect, the book was written by a person who went by the name of Malachi.

Uplifted by the unknown

There was once a young man in the USA who had spent years in and out of foster care. He was alone in his dormitory one Christmas Eve, with all the other children away for Christmas itself. On Christmas morning, someone slipped an envelope under the dormitory door. It contained the equivalent of $250 in today's money—a huge amount for an older teenager essentially living in an orphanage. But that gift, from an unknown stranger, resulted in a complete change of life. Rick Jackson was soon reunited with a Christian foster family—a family he had run away from some while before. Then he attended college, and he began his first business at the age of twenty-one. Some years later, Jackson Healthcare was helping over 5 million patients in the USA. It all began because of an extravagant gift from a stranger. Rick was uplifted by an unknown.

Perhaps we might have a similar experience as we read Malachi—a character who, similarly, is something of an unknown. We think he wrote sometime after 516 BC, when the temple of Solomon was rebuilt following its destruction seventy years earlier. Malachi makes no mention of that long and highly significant rebuilding process, so it seems likely that the temple had been completed some while before Malachi wrote his prophecy. The books of Ezra and Nehemiah rail against corrupt religious leaders, the trivialization of marriage and divorce, lack of social justice and failure to bring proper tithes and offerings to God, and these are many of the issues tackled by Malachi. However, under Ezra and Nehemiah there was a good deal of social reform, which dealt with these issues to a considerable extent at least, but Malachi makes no mention of any such reforms. Thus it seems most likely that Malachi was prophesying shortly before Ezra and Nehemiah, whilst those were still the issues of the day. We know historically that Ezra and Nehemiah began their ministries in 458 and 438 BC respectively. Perhaps, then, Malachi was prophesying sometime in the 470–460 BC period. Aside from that, though, Malachi is unknown. Nevertheless, God has much to say to us through his words; perhaps, like Rick Jackson, we too might be uplifted by an unknown.

When Malachi writes this prophecy, God's people have forgotten all that God has done for them in the past. They are failing to rest in God's promises for their future. Their eyes are firmly fixed on the ground. In short, they are far from God and, at the same time, settled into a comfortable religiosity. Cynicism abounds. It is into this context that God speaks through Malachi.

It could be argued that many in our Western churches are far from God and yet settled into comfortable religiosity. Perhaps some of our churches are places where cynicism abounds. Perhaps our church needs to wake up to the parting of the clouds and the thrusting sword of God's Word.

For many of us, life is very hectic. The storms of life batter us from all sides. Perhaps we have responsibilities towards ailing spouses, parents or friends. Demands from the workplace fill our evenings and weekends as well as our workdays. Our children have incessant needs. Church activities take considerable time. The time pressure is high. In the midst of all that, how can we find the time to read the Bible? How can we prioritize our time with God when we have all these other responsibilities? For some of us, the question might not only be 'How can we read?' but further, 'Why should we read at all?'

Perhaps it will help us to remember that the Bible is God parting the clouds and speaking directly to us through it—that's a great reason for me to prioritize my Bible reading! In the book of Malachi, forty-seven of the fifty-five verses of text are God's direct address to his people in the first person. Perhaps even if only for this reason, we should take particular notice of the words of the final prophet in our Old Testament. Out of everything that demands our time on the horizontal plane, God thunders from above; the Eternal beckons to us amidst our temporary pain. And we ignore God's voice at our peril.

Loving and loathing: the sovereignty of God (1:1–5)

For a number of years, I worked at a private charity boarding school nestled in the heart of the Sussex countryside. The school is known for its distinctive uniform which has remained mostly unchanged since Tudor times. Amongst other things, the pupils have to wear long, dark navy silver-buttoned coats which reach to the floor.

We often laughed when the new bright-eyed year 7 students arrived in September to settle into boarding-school life. They would collect their uniform and, with some help from older pupils, would eventually figure out how to wear it (a task someone once described as learning to solve a Rubik's cube). Once properly dressed, they would walk proudly down the corridor, and then they'd reach the stairs. The boys in my house would start up the stairs, but, virtually to a man, this is where they would have problems. In order to go up the stairs in their uniform, pupils needed to lift the coat up so that they didn't trip over it. Obviously, though, the boys did not arrive at school having learned to lift their skirts before going up stairs, so when they put on their uniform for the first time, they would start up the stairs and fall over.

When we come to Jesus, it is as if we are dressed in new uniform. We are given a robe of righteousness. Finally we begin to understand life the right way up. But as we move into Malachi, we're going to need to lift our skirts as we ascend. The ascent is wonderful, and the views at the top are spectacular. But we need to hitch up our skirts, or we will fall over and, instead of taking in the beauty, we'll find ourselves noses to the dirt.

The book of Malachi is an uncomfortable read. Malachi rails against relaxed religion. He disallows us from resting easy. Through Malachi,

God speaks in a shocking way about himself and his plans, forcing us to sit up and take notice. So Malachi provides us not with leather sofas and warm slippers, but with truth which drives us out of complacency and makes us dive deep into life-changing faith in Almighty God. On a good day, that's exactly where I want to be. On a bad day, that's exactly where I need to be. Whatever my situation, growing in love for God is what benefits me most. So we need to read Malachi with eyes and hearts open to the God who yearns to love us into life.

A heavy burden (1:1)

When I was at university, one of my good friends told me one day that I was 'extremely arrogant'. I think she had been wondering how to say it to me for some time. She knew I needed to hear it, and the need to tell me grew heavy upon her, until eventually she simply said it right out. Initially I was very shocked. I wanted to argue, to defend myself. I did not want to think of myself that way. But as I worked through those words, which must have been hard to say, I realized their truth. I began to recognize my own failings, sinfulness and struggles, and to stop pretending I was some great guy who could help everyone else. I needed help, too. I still do.

Malachi's prophecy begins, 'The oracle of the word of the LORD . . .' Some have argued that, in Hebrew, the word *mesha* (translated 'oracle' by the ESV) just means 'prophecy'. But since it is coupled with the phrase 'the word of the LORD', *mesha* thus understood would be redundant. However, *mesha* can also mean 'burden'. It is the same word that is used to describe the load that a camel or a donkey might carry. The point in this verse, then, is that the word of the Lord can be a heavy burden to bring. Just as when my friend felt the need to tell me what I was like it weighed upon her until it was said, so this word of the Lord ached in Malachi's soul—it was a heavy word which *had to be* proclaimed.

As one commentator points out, when *mesha* is used on eleven occasions in Isaiah, and in a few other places as well, 'it is followed by a prophecy of a threatening nature'.[1] In other words, when *mesha* is used in prophetic material, it often suggests something ominous.[2] This is true in Malachi as well.

Malachi is saying, 'The news is hard, but I must tell you; I am burdened to tell you; I cannot help but tell you of this news.' Many of the prophets had a similar burden to speak God's words to the people, words often involving his judgement. The word *mesha* here therefore alerts us to the fact that this prophecy will probably be about God's judgement.

For a preacher or teacher of the Bible, the word that the Lord brings to his people on a Sunday morning or at the youth club is often a burden— sometimes a heavy burden. But that word *must* be brought. God's word *must* go forth. For all Christians, as we get to know God's word more and more, so we should feel the weight of this burden to share it with others. Oh, that our hearts would burn within us as we bring God's inerrant word to his people! When we seek to introduce someone to Jesus, sometimes the words we need to say seem hard and heavy. But those words *must* be brought; we would be failing in our evangelistic task if we did not give the whole truth. Indeed, unless we bring the whole truth, we bring a distorted gospel, which is really no gospel at all.

But whilst the burden is heavy, it is also a joy. Bearing bad news might be heart-wrenching and agonizing, but the reason for doing so is not simply to condemn; it is to urge people towards repentance and faith in the Lord, the Bringer of life. When my friend called me 'arrogant', the goal was not to crush me, but that I would be changed. Similarly, the goal here in Malachi is not condemnation but justification.

Even as Malachi brings these hard words from God, the intention from the heart of God is to highlight our desperate need and to offer us hope and a future. A man will never reach for a lifeline if he doesn't realize he's drowning. And because of our sinful and wayward hearts, we will never grasp God's rescue if we don't recognize God's wrath. The burden is a joy, because even in highlighting our sin, it spotlights the Saviour who waits centre-stage.

We read and study the words from heaven, not because they are a heavy burden, but because they lift our downcast faces to a stricken Saviour who died in our stead. We have failed, but he has triumphed. We wallow in sin, but he bathes us in righteousness. We are in danger of sinking, but he reaches out and raises us up: 'O you of little faith, why did you doubt?' (Matt. 14:31). We are unable, but he is able.

So in these introductory verses, we are pointed to our sin and are directed to the Saviour for our own salvation. Beyond that, the final goal is that our eyes will see him and we will cry, 'Great is the LORD beyond the border of Israel!' (v. 5). In the final analysis, these heavy words are to drive us in the direction of worship.

We are not simply to see our sickness and desperation and to lie under condemnation. Neither are we merely to turn from our sin to our Saviour, receive his gift of life, and lie back in thankfulness. Rather, we are to see our sin, see our Saviour, and move for ever into worship of the God who is over all, the one who first parted the clouds. We worship him for who he is. Great is the Lord!

Words for the insiders (1:1–5)

Notice in verse 1 that this prophecy is not spoken to the rebellious outsiders, the nations and people around who spare no thought for God and follow after the things of this world. Rather, it is for those inside: 'the word of the LORD to *Israel*.'[3] God's criticism in Malachi is not of his outright opponents, but of those who are supposed to be his own people.

As we'll see, many people considered themselves religious enough. They were doing roughly the right things. But they were not trusting in and seeking after God day by day. The issues that Malachi raises with Israel demonstrate their faithlessness. And it is no different in our twenty-first-century churches. Malachi is going to probe deep into our hearts, and it may hurt us.

As we work through these first five verses, we will ask two questions. First: Does God love? This seems obvious, but it is worth exploring. Second: Does God hate? This seems a shocking idea, but Malachi forces us to consider it. The answers to these two questions lead us inexorably to praise, as we shall see.

How can God love?

Look at how Malachi brings this great burden to God's people. He knows all of Israel's failings and all he will need to challenge them about, so you would think he would say, 'Sort this out, and God will love you again,' or, 'Stop doing that, and God will love you again.' But he doesn't.

Look at verse 2: '"I have loved you," says the LORD.' More literally, he says, 'I have loved and continue to love you.' God is stating right up front that he loves them, despite their rebellious hearts. Malachi's deepest and primary burden is to tell the people that God loves them! Of course, in our day and age, 'God loves you' has somehow become a trite phrase. Somehow, one of the most important truths in all creation, one of the key aspects of God's settled decision towards people—the fact of his love for us—has been undermined and is mocked by the world. But Malachi wants the fact of God's love to be hard-wired into our brains. This is Malachi's primary burden: that we understand the truth that God is *for* us. He *loves* us.

To have another human being love us is a wonderful, stabilizing and joyful thing. How much more glorious, fulfilling, humbling, enabling, stabilizing, encouraging and energizing it is to be loved by God, the Creator and Sustainer of the world!

Sometimes, though, we wonder whether God loves us. I know I can question his love for me when I get something wrong, or when I'm experiencing trials of various kinds.

When I've messed up, been hurtful to someone or got angry when I shouldn't have done, whilst I know theoretically that God loves me, I don't believe that he loves me *at that moment*, because I have sinned. Or I think, 'God doesn't love me as much as he did *before* I did that wrong thing.' But of course, God's love for us does not change in the midst of our sin, nor in the midst of our right service, because his love for us does not depend on us. It depends on God himself. He loves us because he chose to love us. His love is deep, settled, immovable and unconquerable.

I can also begin to question God's love when I am experiencing trials or suffering. The devil's lie is, 'If God loved you, he wouldn't let you go through that trial.' It's a very believable lie if we don't think about it too much. But sometimes we go through trials just because we live in a fallen world; Christians are not immune from that brokenness. Further, Hebrews 12 (reflecting Prov. 3:12) reminds us that God disciplines those he loves. Sometimes we go through trials because God is changing us to be more like him. The trials knock off the rough edges. They shape us, smooth us down and build us to be increasingly better image-bearers of God. In fact, we suffer sometimes not because God *doesn't* love us, but because he *does*! Our suffering should *confirm* his love rather than cause us to question it.

The people to whom Malachi spoke asked the same question: 'How have you loved us?' (v. 2)—or, more explicitly, 'In what ways have you and do you love us?' The same tense is used as in the 'I love you' statement earlier in the verse. The people are in the midst of sinful living, struggling with the usual trials of life, and they ask, 'Does God really love us?'

God's response is fascinating: 'Is not Esau Jacob's brother?' Or, to put it another way, 'Esau was Jacob's brother, wasn't he?' He continues, 'Yet I loved Jacob, but Esau I hated, and I have turned his mountains into wastelands and left his inheritance to the desert jackals' (my paraphrase, vv. 2–3). The people want to know the ways in which God has loved them, and God responds by telling them the ways in which he comes against Esau!

'Jacob I loved, but Esau I hated' is one of the most difficult of God's statements for us to understand, and much has been written about it. But before we get to it, we need to ask why God responds to a question about his love with a focus on Jacob and Esau. It seems, somehow, that the proof of God's love for Jacob is demonstrated in the fact that he chose Jacob but not Esau.

Think about Jacob for a moment. His story is found from Genesis 27 onwards. In these chapters, we discover that Jacob was a deceiver, schemer, thief, liar and coward. He could not be trusted and he did not trust God. He had no moral fibre and no sense of responsibility—at least, not before the end of chapter 32. And yet, equally clearly, God chose Jacob and loved him. What is abundantly clear from the story of Jacob is that God's choice of Jacob did not depend upon Jacob. It was God's sovereign, divine, omnipotent choice to love him. And this is the very point God is making at the end of verse 2. 'How have you loved us?' 'I have loved Jacob.' God's love is a statement of fact, demonstrated in his choice of Jacob.

This is such an encouragement! As we go through the trials and sufferings of this life, it is not because God does not love us. No—he *chose* us, if we're Christians. Whilst we may have no idea of the purpose of our suffering, it does not call into question the love of God, because God chose us to be his own.

The same holds true in the light of our sinfulness, too. We are incapable of living the way God calls us to live. We make mistakes every day. We are wilfully disobedient. We know what we should do and we don't do it; we know what we should not do, but we do it anyway. We speak words that tear down instead of build up. And as for our thought lives, for many of us our thoughts go unnoticed and unchecked. This is where sin really abounds. We are so similar to Jacob. We deceive others and we deceive ourselves. We run from problems. We mess up relationships. We scheme so that others will think well of us. And yet, if we are Christians, then, as for Jacob, God chose us. His love for us is a statement of fact. It is his sovereign, divine, omnipotent choice. Does God love you? Yes!

The Bible is clear that God loves all people: 'For God so loved *the world* . . .' (John 3:16). He provides the air we all breathe, our senses, our experiences of life, the world in which we live, and, for most of us, also the rain and the sunshine, the harvests and the friendships, the families and the opportunities. Indeed, if God were to remove his sustaining hand, we would all die and return to the dust from which we were created.

For the Christian, though, 'Does God love me?' is a question we can equate with 'Are you saved by Jesus? Are you a Christian? Have you submitted yourself entirely to him for your salvation?' If the answer to those latter questions is 'Yes', then the answer to the former question is a given. You experience all the common grace of God's love to all people (there is nothing 'common' about this amazing love of God towards rebellious humankind!). But over and above all that, God chose you before the foundation of the world. Jesus died on your behalf. That is the full extent of his love. In other words, from everlasting to everlasting, God loves you.

We should also note that when Malachi uses the words 'Jacob' and 'Esau', he is not speaking of Jacob and Esau only as individuals. You can see this in the fact that God's response to 'How have you loved us?' is to speak of Jacob, suggesting that 'Jacob' stands for the 'us' in their question. 'Jacob' was a name God used later for the nation of Israel. And God moves directly from talking of Esau the man in 1:3 to Edom the nation descended from the man in 1:4.

It is helpful to see this, because God isn't only saying to those in Malachi's time, 'I loved Jacob—that guy who lived nearly 1,400 years ago.' God is also saying, 'I love you, Israel' (that's the beginning of verse 2). The point is that just as God chose Jacob the man, so he has chosen a people for himself. Malachi is speaking to Israel, God's chosen people. God's love is demonstrated supremely in the fact of his choosing people to be his 'treasured possession', as he puts it in Malachi 3:17.

In many ways, their question 'How have you loved us?' is a sad reflection of their short-sightedness. For over a thousand years he had disciplined them, blessed them, cajoled them, whispered to them, thundered at them, encouraged them, smiled upon them—all to bring them into right living and right standing with himself. Even though many nations had come and gone through their history, God had sustained Jacob.

So when they look back and ask, 'How has God loved us?' we can imagine God sighing deeply. The evidence of his love for them is engraved across every page of their history. In the Old Testament, Jacob/Israel represented God's covenant people on earth—a broadly ethnic people. But now in our time, God's covenant people on earth are not an ethnic people by birth living together in the Middle East, but rather all those who meet in his name across the world. If you're a Christian today, you are part of his people, too. The Jewish heritage, laced as it is with God's sovereign choice and love, is also our heritage.

And we have more:

- We also know of the Messiah, Jesus, who came, lived a perfect life, died in our place, was raised to life and ascended into heaven.
- We know of a Messiah who offers us life, who took our sin upon himself and bestowed on us his righteousness.
- We know of a Messiah who prays for us even now.
- We know the Holy Spirit, who lives within us to enable us to live and to act according to his good purpose.
- And we know we have a future full of the glory of the Lord as we reign with him eternally.

How has God loved us? In so many ways that it almost beggars belief that we ask the question. The fact of his love is engraved on every page of our own personal history, too. So, if we are Christians, then, whilst we are also sinful, God loves us. If our anger overflows regularly and embarrassingly and we can't seem to help it, God loves us. If our children rebel and we feel we have failed as parents, God loves us. If we look back at a particular sin we indulged in perhaps a year, five years, ten years or thirty years ago, and we still carry the shame of it, nevertheless God loves us. If we were or are abused by someone close to us, it is not our fault *and* God still loves us. If we face derision and ridicule, if we cannot cope, if we feel we deserve our pain, nevertheless God loves us. If we are passed over for promotion, God loves us. If we face ongoing physical pain and illness, God is not punishing us—he loves us. If we are bullied at school, college or work, and we give in and join in with the bad language and sexual humour so that we don't stand out, God loves us. If we hunt day by day for a job, but nothing comes up so that we begin to believe we must have nothing to offer, nevertheless God loves us. If we return to the same sin over and over again, trying hard but failing so regularly that the shame of it wears us down, God still loves us. If we are surrounded by people who are more intelligent, more successful, richer, healthier and happier, nevertheless God love us. If we are in depression, wondering whether or not it's worth going on, wondering if anyone would notice if we weren't here any more, God loves us.

How do we know this fact of God's love? Because God's love does not depend on anything in us at all. It rests only on his sovereign and unchangeable will. He *chose* us.

Of course, as Christians, we can't stand proud and say, 'We've been chosen.' We are not worthy of God's choice to save us—we're worthy of God's condemnation. We can only bow humbly and wonderingly and say, 'We've been chosen,' and love him with all our hearts. We are chosen by him regardless of our failings, mess, disobedience and waywardness. His love is not a response to us, but a reflection of himself. The ultimate purpose of God in choosing us is to bring glory to himself. So our role is to bring him glory, which is exactly where Malachi goes when he moves into verse 5: great is the Lord!

A person who is not a Christian is missing out hugely. They do still experience something of God's love expressed every moment of life. They live, move, breathe, eat, drink, and so on, but they live in rebellion against God. Since God created and sustains the universe, even as people oppose him, he sustains them by his powerful word. What love that is! But a not-yet-Christian does not yet experience the depth of God's love. That is only experienced as we love him and know his indescribable love which can never perish, spoil or fade.

So does God love? 'Yes!' says Malachi. God loves all people generally, and chooses some to love particularly. But that's only half the story.

How can God hate?

This part of the first chapter of Malachi is the hardest part. 'I have loved Jacob, but Esau I have hated' (vv. 2–3). Remember that this is God speaking. It raises so many questions. Almighty God, whom we serve if we are Christians, *hated* Esau. How can God hate? The very idea makes us tremble.

We are comfortable with talking about the depth of God's love towards Jacob and his people. Here, though, Malachi seems almost as comfortable discussing the depth of God's hatred toward Esau.

If Malachi had wanted to avoid suggesting that God loves or hates individuals, he could have chosen as examples Israel (the more common name for the nation) and Assyria (who had been defeated by this point, and a name that certainly would not denote an individual). But Malachi doesn't have this exclusively corporate approach. He wants to make the point that God's choice is an individual choice. He uses a highly pointed example of God's sovereign choice: Jacob and Esau. They were twins, with Esau just a few minutes older than Jacob. There was nothing to distinguish them. And yet, before either of them were even born, God chose Jacob over Esau.

The hard truth is that Jacob was chosen by God and Esau was not. Jacob was loved and Esau was hated. This is exactly how Paul uses this verse when he quotes it in Romans 9:13. Paul is illustrating God's sovereign choice in loving one and hating another. God chose Jacob for life and Esau for death. This is not a matter of ranking or priority, or of liking one and liking the other less, as some commentators have it. It is harder than that. This is a yes/no, on/off matter.

So how can we make sense of this? How can the God of love, whom we know a little, hate?

Does God really hate people?

How can *God* really be said to hate? The following verses may help us:
- Psalm 5:5: God hates all who do wrong.
- Psalm 11:5: The Lord 'hates the wicked and the one who loves violence'.
- Proverbs 6:19: God hates the wicked.

This seems to be getting worse, doesn't it? Perhaps the common phrase 'God loves the sinner but hates the sin' turns out to be less biblical than we thought. Perhaps the Bible does not divide the two quite as simply.

We know that God is in opposition to wickedness and sin, and evil generally, and we tend to be comfortable with saying that God hates evil, wickedness and sin. But it seems that Psalm 5:5; 11:5; and Proverbs 6:19 all state that people can stand in open rebellion against God and so he can be said to hate them also. It helps if we recognize that this is not an emotional, guttural hate—some kind of 'feeling' that God has. Rather, this is a settled standing in opposition to a person. If a person is living in rebellion against God (they 'hate' God), then God is in opposition to them (he 'hates' them). Perhaps this is what Paul is saying in Ephesians 2 when he writes that all of us are by nature objects of wrath (Eph. 2:3). God's settled anger stands against our rebellious and sinful hearts.

Think about Esau for a moment. Esau did not trust in God:

- Esau gave up his inheritance for a bowl of stew (Gen. 25:33).
- Esau married two foreign women who caused much grief to his parents (Gen. 26:34–35).
- Esau had murderous intent towards his brother (Gen. 27:41).
- Esau rebelled against his parents and chose to marry a third wife, an idolatrous Canaanite woman, simply to spite his father (Gen. 28:6–9).

We know nothing of the rest of his life, but his heart of rebellion against those who loved him is clear enough.

And so God hated Esau.

The nation that came from Esau was a constant source of harm and trouble to Israel, too. The people of Edom were rebellious and worshipped idols in the same way as the other nations around them. They laughed and ridiculed when Israel was taken into exile. In Isaiah, the name 'Edom' is not only used for that nation but stands for all nations in rebellion against God and Israel. And this is how Malachi uses the name Edom, too: it stands for all those outside of Jacob. These nations were deep in idolatry. They were worshipping parts of God's creation, as if those things (stone, silver or stars) were in charge, rather than the true God of heaven. These people stood in utter rebellion against their Creator. Many of them were involved in ritual sacrifice and prostitution. Sexual immorality was not just considered normal, but was applauded. The sinfulness of Edom and of the other nations around Israel was prevalent and blatant. The result? God hated them. He stood in opposition to them.

It is helpful to compare for a moment these rebellious nations from the time of Malachi with the nations in the Middle East today. We notice right away that all those rebellious nations of Malachi's time are long gone. Whilst some of them survived for a short while, none remain now. God's settled wrath against them resulted in their eventual downfall. But there are still Jews the world over.

Jacob and his posterity stands for those who are part of God's covenant people. Esau and his posterity stands for all those in opposition to God. If we are truly of 'Jacob', we are chosen by God and loved by God. But if we are truly of Esau, we are not chosen by God and we are hated by God. And what happens to us if, like Edom, we live in opposition to God? What does Malachi say (1:2–4)? We may build, make ourselves rich, and so on, but in the end it will all come to nothing. God will eventually turn our work into a wasteland and will pull down what we put up. Our inheritance will be left to the jackals. What we build will be demolished. We will be evermore under the wrath of God against our rebellion.

So Malachi is saying that either we are chosen and loved by God, or we are not chosen by him and are hated by him. Those are the only two possibilities. But there is another vital piece of this puzzle.

Why does God hate people? It is clear from these verses that God chooses to hate people because of their sin. There are not many verses in the Bible expressing God's hatred, but there are no verses in the Bible that express God's hatred without connecting that hatred directly to sin. It is sin that he hates. The hard truth is that he hates people *because of* their sinful rebellious hearts.

Look at Edom here in Malachi 1:4: 'We are shattered but we will rebuild the ruins.' Despite the discipline of God against their sinful ways of life, they still continue to rebel. How does God respond? This is what the Lord Almighty says: 'They may build, but I will tear down, and they will be called "the wicked country", and "the people with whom the Lord is angry for ever."' The point is that God hates Edom because of their wickedness, defiance and refusal to submit.

So it seems that God's hate and God's love are asymmetrical. God hates people because of their sin. God loves people because of his own mercy and free choice. He chooses to love people irrespective of anything in those people. His choice is sovereign, prior, unconnected with our moral uprightness or lack thereof. Before we even came to exist, God chose us only because of his sovereign mercy and grace. Some are hated because of *their* sin and rebellion. Others are loved because of *his* mercy and grace. Why did God hate Esau? Because of his sin. Why does he hate those outside of his people today? Because of their sin. Eternal punishment is deserved. Why does he love Jacob? Because of his own choice.

Why didn't God hate Jacob, too?

Perhaps, then, the question is not 'Why did God hate Esau?' Hating Esau was just and right because it reflected God's justice and holiness. Rather, the more important question is 'Why didn't God hate Jacob, too?' Yes, Esau was rebellious—but so was Jacob. More broadly, not only were the nations around Israel rebellious, but the nation of Israel also was rebellious, and repeatedly so. We see this time and again throughout the Old Testament. The apostle Paul reminds his readers that 'all have sinned and fall short of the glory of God' (Rom. 3:23). If it is right that Esau is hated for his sin, and that the nations around Israel are hated for their sin, should not Jacob likewise be hated? Shouldn't the nation of Israel be hated? Shouldn't we *all* be hated?

But Malachi writes here that somehow, not because of any merit in Jacob, God *loved* him. Somehow, whilst there was no merit in Israel, God *loved* them. One of the Bible's key messages for Christians is that though *we* ought to be *hated* by God, God chose instead to *love* us. There is nothing in us to merit it; he simply chose to love us.

God's message in this part of Malachi is that in some strange way God's hatred of Edom is proof of his love for Jacob. Notice how God explains his love for Jacob by discussing the judgement he has wrought on Edom: 'I have loved Jacob but Esau I have hated. I have laid waste his hill country ...' (vv. 2–3).

The outcome of God's judgement against Edom is different from the outcome of his judgement against Israel. For Edom, God's judgement brings eternal ruin ('the people with whom the LORD is angry for ever', v. 4); but for Jacob, God's judgement—even when that judgement is severe—is a purifying fire resulting in eternal salvation. The nations around Israel fell and disappeared, to be remembered only in the history books. This was true not only for Edom but also for the successive empires of Assyria, Babylonia, Greece and Rome: all of them eventually fell and disappeared from the earth. So, whilst God's judgement against Jacob and his judgement against Edom may look very similar, the outcomes are very different. Israel faced war and the people were carried off into captivity, but they were not exiled for ever: God's people returned. The Jews continue even today, and some have come to trust in Jesus, too. God's judgement against his people was a purifying fire, not an eternal fire.

Across the world, everyone experiences pain, trials, suffering and difficulties. Jacob did; Esau did. Israel did; Edom did. God's people do; those in opposition to God do. But there is a difference between the sufferings of those who are followers of Jesus and the sufferings of those who are not. The difference lies in the outcome of those sufferings. Do those trials terminate in destruction or in eternal life? Is this 'judgement unto death' or 'discipline unto life'?

How could God continue to love Jacob in light of Jacob's ongoing rebellion and breaking of the covenant? He could, because the ultimate destruction Jacob deserved was poured out on Jesus at the cross so that Jacob might experience the love Jesus' obedience merited.

In the midst of our own trials, however hard they are, if we are Christians there is great confidence to be gleaned from these verses. This is not a wrathful God standing against us—although that is what we deserve. No, this is a gracious God who loves us and is *for* us. So these trials stand as a means to an end—a purifying fire, preparing us for our eternal home. They are to point us away from ourselves to God. They are to direct us to our Saviour. They are to grow our thankfulness for his death on our behalf.

Overall, then, the contrast here in the first section of Malachi is that either we are chosen by God (we are 'God's elect' as the Bible puts it, e.g. John 15:16; Acts 13:48; Rom. 9:15–16; Eph. 1:1, 4–5; 1 Thes. 1:4; 1 Peter 1:1) and part of God's covenant people saved only through the grace of God and the work of Jesus on the cross; or we are part of Esau, standing in opposition to God and hated by him. Even more starkly, God did not speak these words to Edom, to the nations around Israel who were against them and against God. God was not saying to Edom, 'I hate you.' No; these words of opposition were directed at those who were meant to be God's people, Israel. The modern-day equivalent is the church. These words are therefore directed at each of us who sit in church each Sunday. They are serious words.

Perhaps we are 'doing what is right in the eyes of Christians'. But being part of ethnic Israel (and, likewise, being part of the visible church) is no proof that we're part of God's chosen people. Not all who attend church are chosen by God. Some only *look* like it.

The wonderful news about Jesus flies up to meet us here, though. There is one way to know for sure that we are part of God's elect, his chosen people. We can submit to Jesus as Lord, seek his forgiveness, ask for his presence and commit to him from now on. If we do that, we are part of God's chosen people. His settled love is upon us.

Does God loathe? Yes. Look at the cross. See God's anger and hatred coming down upon Jesus as he took our sin upon himself. God hates sin that much. His settled anger against sinners (me and you) is poured out on Jesus. But does God love? Yes. Look at the cross. See his love, satisfying God's anger against sin on your behalf. The cross highlights both aspects of the character of God. Hatred of sinners: settled wrath against all that is unholy; hatred because of sin. But also love: love of those he has chosen;

love of his people, dependent on the heart of God alone; love that takes the wrath upon himself to offer freedom and life to you and me. 'While we were still sinners, Christ died for us' (Rom. 5:8). That is how much he loves us.

Praise

Where should this lead us? It should lead us to praise: 'You shall say, "Great is the LORD beyond the border of Israel!"' (v. 5). For Malachi, both God's love and God's hatred should lead us to praise.

It is hard to see how this works, isn't it? There is no joy in the suffering of our fellow people; indeed, as Christians, are we not called to come alongside those who suffer? Jesus himself conducted much of his public ministry in the rescue and restoration of those who were suffering.

It is helpful to think back to one of the defining moments of Israel's history: the exodus from slavery in Egypt as recorded in Exodus 4–12. In Egypt, Pharaoh was in deep rebellion against God. Even as God brought plagues upon the city, Pharaoh continued to rebel. Great suffering filled the land because of his (and, we assume, the people's) rejection of the one true God. The result was God's final judgement. All the firstborn of Egypt died at God's hand because of the people's refusal to worship him and Pharaoh's refusal to let God's people go and worship him. The judgement was as awful as it was profound. But the whole series of events led to great praise, from the song of Miriam onwards. There were two primary reasons for this resulting praise.

First, not only did the ten plagues show that Pharaoh had no power compared with the power of God, but more importantly they demonstrated that the gods of Egypt had no power either. These plagues displayed the wonder and power of God over and against all the gods of Egypt. The Egyptians worshipped the god of the Nile (Hapi), so when the Nile turned to blood, it showed that the god of the Nile was no god. They worshipped Heqet, a god of fertility depicted as a frog, but after the plague of frogs, there were great heaps of dead frogs stinking out the city; the god they had worshipped was no god at all. Each plague demonstrated the powerlessness of the gods of Egypt. The God of heaven is powerful and alive; those Egyptian gods were powerless and dead. The judgements of the plagues were strong and horrible, but they demonstrated the majesty of the one true God and so brought him praise.

Second, the result of judgement upon God's enemies was freedom for God's people. As we know, the exodus events pointed forward to the coming of Jesus, who, himself as the firstborn, would die so that God's people (you and me) could be rescued from their sin and brought back into relationship with the living God. That is arguably the most powerful reason for praise.

So as God brings his judgement upon his enemies, it leads his people eventually to praise. The Israelites would have found the plagues terrible and frightening, but those experiences led them to freedom and so to praise. And as God's judgement was carried out on Edom, so God's people should move to praise. Our God is an awesome God.

In the midst of his suffering, Job cried out, 'Though he slay me, I will hope in him' (Job 13:15). He recognized the sovereignty of God. He knew that all the pain he was experiencing was at the behest of God, and that somehow this suffering was for his good. So Job continued to hope in God. That is a big challenge to all of us amidst the trials of life. Not only is God *allowing* this trial to happen to me, but he is also orchestrating the whole thing for my good. He is sovereign.

Here in Malachi, it is the suffering God has brought on his enemies in time past that leads the people of God to praise. Ultimately, as we look back across history, we look to the place of ultimate suffering—the condemnation of Jesus on the cross, as he experienced first-hand the wrath of God against all of our sin. That suffering leads us only to praise and worship.

The mercy and love of God are brought into stark relief as we see the judgement of God we deserve. Over and over again, particularly in the book of Revelation, we see God's people praising him because he has brought judgement down upon his enemies. Personally, I struggle with this truth. I struggle to have joy in God when his judgement comes on others. My limited understanding of the horror of hell sometimes makes it more difficult to bring God glory for his justice. But I think that's because repeatedly I fail to understand the depths of my own depravity— my own sinful heart. Repeatedly I fail to realize how serious is my sin. Perhaps if I grasped how horrific it is to rebel against my Creator by negating his truthfulness through my half-truths, negating his love by my anger, or negating his warmth towards outsiders by my selfishness— perhaps if I had a deeper grip on the horror of my own sin, I would then find glorifying God for coming against sin a rather easier concept.

> And can it be that I should gain
> An interest in the Saviour's blood?
> Died he for me, who caused his pain;
> For me, who him to death pursued?[4]

My sin drives the nails through his wrists.

> Amazing love! how can it be
> That you, my God, should die for me!

If I realized the depths of my sin, I would find it far easier to live in praise of him who chose me despite my depravity. It would be easier to praise him who paid the ultimate, unimaginable price for my sin by giving his life for me on the cross. The magnitude of God's mercy displayed at the cross as Jesus took the horror of my sin upon himself is wonderful indeed. So, as Paul expounds this part of Malachi in Romans 9, surely he is right to urge us to wonder at 'the riches of [God's] glory' made known to the objects of his mercy (Rom. 9:23).

Conclusion

We cannot tell from the outside who is and who is not part of the true people of God. But if you are not a Christian, you remain in rebellion against God, and that is a dangerous place to be. Don't play at religion. Don't pretend to be a Christian. Don't just 'do the right thing' in the eyes of others. Instead, submit to him as your King. Turn to him. Come asking for his forgiveness. Come seeking life. And then the Author of life will bring life and light to you even now as you read.

The only way to be sure you are chosen by God is to submit to him in faith and hope, asking for his forgiveness and trusting in him for your salvation. Those of us who trust in him will join together and sing in reverence and awe: we are chosen and loved by Almighty God. Perhaps we could put it this way: if you submit, then you know you are chosen; but if you refuse to submit, this confirms that you are not.

If you are a Christian, remember: God *chose* you. He loves you despite what you deserve and more than you could ever imagine. You do not suffer because he hates you; your suffering *will* lead to glory and all joy. So take heart: he *loves* you! He loves you! He loves you!

Notes

1 John Peter Lange, Philip Schaff and Joseph Packard, *A Commentary on the Holy Scriptures: Malachi* (Bellingham, WA: Logos Bible Software, 2008), p. 7.
2 'It appears evident from Jer. 23:38, that this word was regarded as ominous.' John Calvin, 'Lecture One Hundred and Sixty-Ninth', in John Calvin and John Owen, *Commentaries on the Twelve Minor Prophets* (Bellingham, WA: Logos Bible Software, 2010), p. 461.
3 All emphasis in Scripture quotes has been added.
4 Charles Wesley, 1738; modernized version © Jubilee Hymns Ltd.

How should we approach the King? (1:6–2:9)

When Esther went to speak to King Ahasuerus, she knew that it was a dangerous mission: 'If any man or woman goes to the king inside the inner court without being called, there is but one law—to be put to death, except the one to whom the king holds out the golden sceptre so that he may live' (Esth. 4:11). Esther had not been called, yet her people's situation was so terrible that she approached the king anyway. She went with deep respect, giving him honour and bowing before him, and King Ahasuerus responded by holding out the golden sceptre and listening to Esther. Of course, there were many ways she could have approached the king, but most of them would have ended in her death. So the way she approached the king was vital, not just to the success of her request, but also to her own life.

As Malachi moves into this next section, he raises a simple but vital question: How should we approach the King? Malachi is not discussing interactions with a temporary monarch, but rather how God's people should come before God, a far greater king than Ahasuerus. What is the proper way to bring him worship? Malachi's question remains relevant today as we think about how we should approach God. The question refers not only to our corporate gatherings on a Sunday but also to the way in which we live our daily lives.

It is hardly surprising that God, the Almighty Creator King, specifies how he is to be approached. Adam and Eve's first sons, Cain and Abel, reflected a wrong and a right way to worship God. Prophetically, the one who offered acceptable worship (Abel) was the one whose blood was shed by the other (Cain) (Gen. 4:8). Hundreds of years later, as the enslaved people prepared to leave Egypt under Moses, they prepared for the plague of the death of the firstborn by following very specific instructions regarding their final meal of lamb and unleavened bread (see Exod. 12). The blood of the innocent one (the lamb) was to stand in place of the death of the guilty ones (the people). Later, at Mount Sinai, the people were given very specific instructions not only about the construction of the tabernacle in which God would dwell, but also about how they were to approach God in that tabernacle—an approach in which the sacrifice of the innocent one (lamb, goat, bull, bird) was to stand in the place of the guilty one (the worshipper). This concept of the innocent taking the place of the guilty is a recurring theme of acceptable worship.

Notice that the knowledge of what constitutes acceptable worship is knowledge given by God himself. God is the one who prescribes what is acceptable and what is not. It was God who judged Abel's offering as acceptable rather than Cain's (Gen. 4:4–5). God was the one who told Moses, 'Take your sandals off your feet, for the place on which you are standing is holy ground' (Exod. 3:5). God was the one who prescribed the way in which the Israelites were to perform the Passover (Exod. 12). God was the one who explained the construction and use of the tabernacle. It is the words of God alone that describe and define acceptable worship.

I remember once attending a supposedly Christian service during which the vicar announced that he was going to read from the Qur'an instead of from the Bible. He stated that there are some great truths in the Qur'an, and then proceeded to read from it. I was shocked.

Now, it could be noted that every person is made in the image of God. Therefore, whilst every aspect of every person is tainted by sin and warped from its original design, something of the image of God will come through as we think, speak and act. We would therefore expect that things written down could well contain truth—things that are right and good—albeit mixed with other things that are not reflective of God at all (quite the reverse, in many cases). Therefore, the statement 'There are some great truths in the Qur'an' is not inherently blasphemous; it is likely that some of God's true light does shine through the text, simply due to its human authorship. So the problem with reading from the Qur'an in a worship service is not that the Qur'an contains no truth at all, but rather that the Qur'an was thereby seen as equally truthful as the Bible. This idea is certainly blasphemous. The only one who may prescribe what constitutes acceptable worship is God himself. So, whilst the Qur'an may contain truth, the Bible *is* truth—infallible and inerrant truth spoken by the lips of the one true Creator and Sustainer of all things, God himself (2 Tim. 3:15–16). Any wisdom to be found in the Qur'an will be an admixture— truth and error intertwined (that is why relying on such wisdom is inherently dangerous). But the Bible as it was originally given is pure truth. To return to a former analogy, the Bible is God parting the clouds and speaking to his people.

The reading and study of the Bible prescribes and informs acceptable worship; indeed, it is in that study that we discover God, meet with God and are changed by God. In the pages of the Bible ('God's Word') we find the blood of the innocent One (Jesus) shed in place of the guilty ones (us). As Paul wrote so conclusively in Romans 3, the chief advantage of being a Jew was that the Jews were entrusted with the 'very words' of God (Rom. 3:2 NIV; 'oracles of God' in the ESV). In B. B. Warfield's seminal work on the authority of the Bible, he spends a chapter dealing with *logia*, the Greek term behind the translation 'very words' in Romans. Of this word he concludes, 'It means, not "words" barely, simple "utterances", but distinctively "oracular utterances", divinely authoritative communications, before which men stand in awe and to which they bow in humility: and this high meaning is not merely implicit, but is explicit in the term. . . . It characterises the utterances to which it is applied as emanations from God.'[1]

What Paul was saying in Romans 3, then, was that the Jews' chief advantage was that they had the words of God himself—'authoritative communications' from on high (Paul is referring to the Old Testament, of course). This was true of no other people group and no other religion until the arrival of Christianity. Neither the Vedas, the Qur'an, the Guru Granth Sahib, the New World Translation nor any other supposedly sacred book is truly and exclusively from God. Only the Bible—the Old and New Testaments as originally given—are truly and exclusively from God. Only the Bible is divinely authoritative communication.

Reading and studying the Bible in our corporate worship *is*, however, perilous. But this is not because there may be some error within the Bible; rather, it is because there *is no error*! These words can turn your life upside-down; they can challenge you, bring you to your knees and raise your heart to the Eternal, making you willing to give up everything for the joy of knowing and seeking after the Lord himself!

In our passage, Malachi expresses his horror at the unacceptable worship practised and encouraged by the leaders of the church: they are approaching the King in the wrong way, which is not only disrespectful but also perilous. Anyone who is leading God's people must work diligently to 'rightly [handle] the word of truth' (2 Tim. 2:15). And for those of us 'in the pew', we cannot—we *must* not—assume the accuracy of what is being taught; remember that Paul commended the Bereans for examining the Scriptures daily to see whether or not the teaching they were receiving was true (Acts 17:11).

So is the Word of God our focus—that Word which alone points us to the blood of the innocent One (Jesus) in place of the guilty (us)?

The structure of Malachi

A repeating pattern underlies the structure of the book of Malachi. This pattern is as follows: (a) God states something; (b) his people challenge his statement; and then (c) God expands on his statement and describes the judgement that will come unless things change. The book of Malachi comprises six such disputations between God and his people.

In the previous chapter, we examined the first of these six disputes, which unfolded in this way. In Malachi 1:2a, the Lord says, 'I have loved you.' This is God stating something. Verse 2 continues, 'But you say, "How have you loved us?"'—this is God's people challenging his statement. And then, in 1:2c–5, God responds and expands on his statement, describing the judgement that will come.

Usually, it is the question 'how' which signals that a new dispute has begun. Here in 1:6 we read, 'You . . . show contempt for my name.' The people respond, 'How have we shown contempt for your name?' (NIV; notice that v. 7 contains a similar question, so that this second dispute has a double beginning). The reason why in this chapter we are covering so many verses (1:6–2:9) is simply because these eighteen verses form the second disputation in Malachi.

The priests' polluted offerings

We will begin by reminding ourselves of the platform from which God speaks through Malachi, before exploring in detail Malachi's strong words about unacceptable worship—its reality, essence, roots and results. Finally, we will highlight God's words about what constitutes acceptable worship of him.

The platform of love

In the first five verses of Malachi, we saw that Malachi, a messenger of God, was speaking to the people of Israel, God's covenant people. We saw in the previous chapter that, whilst he is going to give a stark and uncomfortable prophecy, he began with words of central importance in verse 2: essentially, 'God says, "I love you."' It is from this foundational platform of his love for his people that God launches a burdensome diatribe against them through the prophet Malachi. They have failed in a myriad ways in life, and Malachi's words are designed to cut to the heart. But the launchpad for the message is God's love.

As Christians in our day, as we read these words of God through Malachi, we must hold fast to the fact that the basis of the hard words written is God's love for us, too. As we ourselves face this diatribe, we would sink into despair were it not for the knowledge of the certainty of God's love for us. The purpose of these words is not condemnation; rather, because of his great love for us, we can be sure that these words are designed that we might turn back to the Lord and experience afresh his love.

Remember: Malachi's focus is not upon those outside the church doors, but upon those within them. In Malachi's time, there were serious problems in the congregation. Perhaps there are serious problems in our congregations, too, or in our youth clubs, our seniors' ministries or our twenties to thirties groups. If so, God speaks to us through Malachi. In fact, he challenges us in every aspect of life. Through this prophet, the words of God to the priests hit home to Christians generally and to church leaders in particular. The words given here are real life, but they are gritty. This is not a 'Let's settle back in our chairs and think about our day' message, but rather, 'God's word is coming at you—are you ready?'

The wrong way to approach the King

The reality of unacceptable worship

When Moses was up Mount Sinai, God revealed to him a whole series of detailed instructions about how the people of God were to come before him in worship. As we read through Exodus, it is obvious that we must not approach God in an off-hand, off-the-cuff way. There is an acceptable way to approach him. But as we read through the Old Testament, we find repeated occasions when God's people did *not* approach him in the right way. This remains true in Malachi: unacceptable worship is a reality amongst God's people.

Is it a reality amongst God's people in the church today, too? Do I approach Sunday morning in the right way, recognizing that I am coming before the one and only all-powerful God of heaven who exists in perfect holiness and love? How often do I approach Sunday morning services with the mindset of wondering whether I'm going to get anything out of them for myself? Perhaps, like me, you've heard people explain that they are leaving a particular church because it no longer satisfies their needs.

Surely we should meet together as the people of God not to satisfy our own needs, but to come both tremblingly and joyfully to our only wise God and Saviour, offering him our worship and wanting to sit at his feet. He is the God who loves us *and* he is the mighty God of justice and truth. At the end of the day, the local church exists not to meet our needs, but to worship the living God.

If we want to come before God in the right way, the words of Malachi in this second disputation are vital. First, he answers some key questions concerning the root of unacceptable worship. Second, he explains how to move from worship that is unacceptable to God to worship that is acceptable, a 'pleasing aroma' to him (e.g. Gen. 8:21; Exod. 29:18, 25, 41; Lev. 1:9, 13, 17; 2:2).

The ancient Middle Eastern culture was built around shame and honour. In this milieu, the ground of any relationship, business, affiliation, work ethic or progression was honour. You had to ensure that you retained and built the honour of your family, the honour of your society and, to a lesser degree, the honour of yourself.[2] In our Western world (which we could, perhaps, describe as a guilt culture), we can learn something from a shame culture. For example, when considering a particular action or spoken word, the typical guilt-culture question is, 'Is it right or wrong to do this?', with the underlying thought, 'Will I feel guilty if I am found out?' The question about right and wrong looks for laws which say 'yes' or 'no' (and if 'no', carrying out the action incurs individual guilt for that action). But the question about honour looks at Jesus and asks whether or not an action or word would bring shame upon

God and his family. Remember the form of prayer Jesus taught to his disciples: 'Our Father in heaven, hallowed [honoured] be your name.'

The 'Is it right or wrong?' question encourages a rule-book approach to Christian living. But the 'Will it honour Jesus?' question pushes us away from legalism, because it focuses on relationship. And relationship is the central point of the Christian faith: relationship with Creator God.

As we look at this part of Malachi, notice that God focuses on the leaders. The priests were the religious leaders at the temple, but they were not only that; they were also the leaders of the people more generally. They would be consulted about how to raise a family, how to manage a business or how to resolve a legal problem. In some churches even today, especially in the Pentecostal tradition, the pastor is still called upon as an expert in every area of life. Some members of those congregations would never consider getting a mortgage without consulting their pastor. The reason why Malachi focuses on the leaders is that if there is a problem in the gathering of God's people, the leaders should be the first port of call. As go the leaders, so go the people.

Leadership is a huge responsibility, so we must pray for our leaders: for our elders; for the Sunday school teachers leading our children; for the fathers leading their families; for the students leading their school, college or university Christian Unions; for those leading in the ministries of the church; for those leading missionary ministries beyond the local church. And if you're one of those leaders, pray for those under your ministry, and listen humbly to the words of Malachi; we all have much to learn here.

The essence of unacceptable worship (1:6–14)

We begin, then, in Malachi 1:6. Malachi is clear about the problem: the people of Israel have remembered that they are 'a people', but they have forgotten the One to whom they belong. They do not honour God, so God speaks to them first of all about showing contempt for his name.

Then comes the question, 'How have we despised your name?' This lets us know we are into a new disputation.

God responds immediately to this question. How have they despised his name? They have placed defiled food on his altar (vv. 7–8). But why was this such a huge problem? When so many other things were wrong amongst God's people (including idolatry), why is defiled food on the altar the very first thing God calls to their attention?'

The purpose of the altar was to bring sacrifices to God which he would accept as atonement for sin. Of course, it was not that the blood of a sheep or a goat could take away sin, but rather the animal sacrifices pointed forward to the final sacrifice of our Lord Jesus himself, the sacrifice which *would* take away sin. The Word of God highlights repeatedly the death of the innocent on behalf of the guilty. God chose to accept the blood of the sheep or goat as atonement for their sin in light of the coming sacrifice of Jesus.

Thus, the altar was meant to be a place of recognizing the seriousness of sin and the depths of human depravity, and of seeking full atonement and forgiveness through unblemished sacrifice. But in Malachi's day, God's people were placing defiled food on the altar. Why would they do this? I think there were a few reasons.

First, using imperfect animals was more economical. If those animals were kept and sold later on, they would not bring in as much money as would unblemished livestock. So, if the priests were happy to sacrifice these less-wanted animals (in practical terms, sacrificing them meant giving them to the priests), perhaps people could do their duty to God, get the forgiveness they wanted, but without having to give away too much. In other words, sacrificing an imperfect animal rather than a perfect one was less costly to the worshipper.

Second, the priests would benefit from this arrangement, too. If the priests did not have exacting standards for the offerings brought, that might encourage the people to bring more offerings. Since the priests gained their food from the offerings brought, the result of people bringing more offerings would be that the priests would have an abundance of meat to eat. In other words, both the people and the priests benefited from blemished animals being brought to the altar.

But the problem was that God's stipulations for sacrifice were clear: only perfect animals were allowed. There were good reasons for this. First of all, God is not interested in unsacrificial 'sacrifices'. When the poor widow placed two pennies in the offering (Luke 21:1–4), she was praised: this was a highly sacrificial offering. But when the rich give far more, they are not praised, because their offering is not sacrificial. It doesn't *cost* them. So the point here is that if I'm going to sacrifice to God, it needs to be a sacrificial act; it needs to cost me something.

Even more importantly, the Old Testament sacrificial system was designed to point us to Jesus. It was meant to be a picture of the one true, perfect and final sacrifice made on our behalf.

Two elements of salvation required a perfect Saviour:

- In order to pay the full price for our sin, the sacrifice of a perfect substitute was required. If the sacrifice was of an imperfect person, that person would need to pay for their own imperfection and would thus be unable to pay for the imperfection of others. In order to take upon himself the wrath and judgement of God that we deserve, the Saviour had to be morally perfect.
- In order for us to receive perfect righteousness in place of our sinful lives, a perfect life needed to be lived. If we are to receive perfect substitutionary obedience, the Saviour needed to have lived a life of perfect righteousness.

In other words, both the active obedience (a perfect substitutionary life lived) and the passive obedience (a perfect substitutionary death died) of the Saviour were required for salvation. He took our sin, which was only possible because he was perfect. He gave us his righteousness, which was only useful because he was perfect. So, because of the requirement of

Chapter 2

perfection in our Saviour, there was a requirement for perfection in the offerings at the altar. For that reason, imperfect animals were unacceptable for sacrifice. Because the final once-for-all sacrifice had to be a perfect one, the foreshadowing of that sacrifice also had to be perfect.

Sadly, the people in Malachi's day had forgotten the purpose of the sacrifices. They did not know the One to whom they pointed. The people needed forgiveness, as we all do, but they were offering sacrifices that weren't sacrificial, so forgiveness could not come.

In our day, we know that forgiveness comes only through repentance and faith in Jesus, the One sacrificed on our behalf. We don't gain forgiveness by offering sacrifices as they were required to do in the Old Testament. But we *do* gain forgiveness by offering our bodies as living sacrifices, holy and pleasing to God; this is *our* spiritual act of worship (Rom. 12:1).

In the Old Testament, they offered sacrifices regularly, reflecting the perfect sacrifice that was one day to come. For the New Covenant people of God, we offer ourselves regularly, reflecting the perfect sacrifice that has already come. If we hold back, if we offer only parts of our daily lives, if we offer less than our whole bodies—then our worship is unacceptable, just as the worship was unacceptable in Malachi's day. We are offering a blemished sacrifice. Forgiveness comes through giving ourselves wholly and utterly to our Creator. Freedom, light, joy and life come only through the offering of our whole being.

God pushes the point further in 1:8–9. He effectively says, 'You wouldn't offer these animals to your governor!' In other words, these animals are blemished, so it would be insulting to offer them to the governor. What effrontery, then, to offer such animals to God! The people to whom Malachi writes offer to the God of heaven what they would not dream of offering to a mere man! And it gets worse: they present sacrifices that are not sacrificial, and then ask God to be gracious and forgive them and accept them anyway (v. 9). Paul decries this attitude: 'Are we to continue in sin that grace may abound? By no means!' (Rom. 6:1–2). Such an attitude is shameful.

The purpose of the sacrifices was forgiveness and acceptance from God. But they were offering sacrifices in contravention of God's law; in other words, they were trying to get forgiveness for their sin in a sinful way. The result of their sacrifice, thus, was not forgiveness, but further guilt!

Perhaps this is a little like the person who attends church on occasion or gives money to the homeless, thinking that this should be enough to get them into God's 'good books'. If we do this, we forget that the Lamb of God has only one Book of Life, and a person's name is written in that book only if they have responded positively to the perfect sacrifice of Jesus. A right response to his perfect sacrifice is to offer acceptable worship: the giving of our lives to God. Church attendance, charitable giving, prison-visiting or 'decent behaviour' will never get us to heaven.

In 1:10, God is adamant: such blemished sacrifices will not do. In effect, he says, 'My name is to be respected, revered, honoured, upheld, because I am utterly holy, perfect, just and true. If you do not seek forgiveness as I have laid out, you shame me.' To offer blemished sacrifices in this way is to suggest that God is less than perfect. It suggests he'll be happy with a half-hearted approach—'He'll be all right with it.' But he's not. Why? Because to allow his name to be upheld as less than perfect and less than holy is to profane utterly the name of the Almighty. It is to throw what is right to the wind. God utters his condemnation in 1:14: 'Cursed be the cheat . . . ' God is saying, 'I will spit you out of my mouth.' The priests and people may have persuaded themselves that God would be OK about their faulty offerings, but Malachi is clear: God is *not* pleased!

There is another reason for doing sacrifices in the right way. Perfect sacrifices show the glory of God to the surrounding nations. One of the reasons why the people of God exist is to display the glory of God to others, so that they also will come to know him for themselves. Part of God's promise to Abraham was that through his offspring all nations would be blessed (Gen. 12:3). Here in Malachi is the same idea. Look again at 1:14: God is 'a great King, . . . and [his] name will be feared among *the nations*.' Here again is this 'beyond Israel' focus that we first found in 1:5: 'Great is the LORD beyond the border of Israel!' In 1:14 his 'name' is to be 'feared [honoured, revered] among the nations' because he is pure, right, holy and just. Ultimately, the purpose of sacrifice and forgiveness is the glory of God's name: his *honour*.

When God says, 'I am a great King,' he is not just saying, 'Out of all the kings, I am a great one.' No, in the language of the day he is saying, 'I am *the* great King, and all other kings and peoples are under me.' The people of God had forgotten that the Lord Almighty is King of all the world.

One example of unacceptable worship in the twentieth and twenty-first centuries is liberalism. Some churches have slipped from their grip on gospel truth, on that Reformation cry, 'Scripture alone'. The liberal church refuses to say that the Bible in its entirety is God's true and infallible word. The church starts to say that Jesus isn't the only way to God, but that some might be saved as Muslims, Hindus, and so on— hence reading from the Qur'an in a 'Christian' service. And we find milder forms of liberalism all around us. There are so many funerals, for example, at which the person speaking gives the impression that everyone will get to heaven and we have nothing to worry about. This is a hollow comfort made with a needle which inoculates against truth and injects poison.

Where does this liberalism lead? Look at 2:9, where God says, 'I have caused you to be despised and humiliated before all the people, because you have not followed my ways but have shown partiality in matters of the law' (NIV). The drive towards liberalism is urged by the pressure of the prevailing culture, and, over time, some churches capitulate. They redefine marriage, gender, tolerance, truth. But it is interesting to note that the world's response to this liberalized church is not to embrace it and endorse it, despite its now more acceptable message (as the world sees it). Instead, they mock it. The church has become, above all else, an institution worthy only of parody and ridicule. Church leaders who have given in to secularism and fudged on gospel truth and moral issues are now paraded with common humour. Sadly, even those who have refused to give in to the prevailing culture nevertheless find themselves mocked along with them. We need to pray hard for ourselves and for our leaders, that we would find ways to stand on the truth and to shine God's light into the dark corners of our culture.

Look at 1:11. In this verse, God mentions his 'name' three times. He states that his name will be 'great'—a stark contrast with the way the priests defame his name with their sacrifices. It is a statement by the God of heaven that he *will* be worshipped across the world one day, in all nations. *He* will be worshipped. Not some other god, and not some other way; no, *he*—the God who speaks in Malachi—*his* name will be great.

How much do I stand against liberalism? God castigates Israel for their unacceptable worship, and he also challenges us: Is our adoration acceptable to God? Do we make acceptable sacrifices, or do we go for unsacrificial sacrifices because of the human benefits? Do the leaders of our churches work diligently to bring God's word to the people every week, or do they think, 'That'll do'? Do they give of themselves in thinking through services, music, prayer, and so on, or do they settle for quick fixes and rushed-off ideas, forgetting the majesty of the God we all serve?

And if you are one who leads (whether individuals or small groups), do you lead well, offering of yourself things that are sacrificial? Or do you 'make do', lest your sacrifices be too costly for you? Do we sniff contemptuously and say, 'What a burden' (see 1:13), or do we kneel in awe, knowing that the great burden of our sin was borne by Jesus, who shouldered it as he climbed the hill to Calvary? For all Christians, do we delight in the privilege of serving, or do we complain because it's too hard?

These are important questions for us to ask of ourselves, whether or not we are leaders. The leaders here in Malachi's day were not willing to admonish the people for bringing faulty sacrifices, and that's why God admonishes them in 2:1. But it was the ordinary people—people with jobs outside the temple (the labourers, financiers, entrepreneurs, academics, and so on)—who first brought these imperfect animals to the priests for the priests to sacrifice. It is easy to blame the leaders for not admonishing the people, but the people were the ones bringing the faulty sacrifices in the first place, so they are to be admonished also.

Do *we* try to bring unsacrificial sacrifices? Do *we* 'do a bit' instead of a lot, hoping it'll do? Do *we* serve wholeheartedly, seeking for God's name to be honoured? Do *we* do all things for the glory of God, or do we just want to keep up appearances? Might there be unacceptable worship in our churches, too?

The root of unacceptable worship

Malachi 1:6–2:9 includes the words 'the LORD Almighty' or 'the LORD of hosts' ten times. The phrase means 'the Lord of the armies'. This expression is found in Psalm 24 and it emphasizes God's sovereignty and omniscience. It highlights the transcendence of God, and it is emphasized repeatedly for the simple reason that the people have forgotten it!

There is a clear, solemn warning here to those who are in the church building, those within the visible church: recognize the true Messenger, Jesus himself, who gave himself for us. Submit to his leadership as your great High Priest. Then, if we are committed to him as Lord, we can hear the words, 'Well done, good and faithful servant.' In Malachi, the leaders had forgotten who God was; that was the problem. And this is the root of unacceptable worship: forgetting the One we are worshipping. We forget how momentous he is. We forget his majesty, his mystery, his mastery, his might, his magnificence, his matchlessness, his mercy. He is the Lord Almighty.

What is the result of this forgetfulness? Malachi turns here next.

The result of unacceptable worship (2:1–3, 8–9)

If a child dishonoured their family in the ancient Near East, the family would seek to regain their honour by expelling the child from the family. Further, an honourable family would be *expected* to do this in response to the shame brought upon them by their offspring. This is why the Parable of the Prodigal Son (Luke 15:11–32) is so astounding. According to the prevailing culture, the father should have disowned his son. But instead he does the opposite: he welcomes him back by throwing a celebratory party!

Back in Malachi's time, priests who brought dishonour and shame to their Father and Master should have expected their own humiliation. They should have expected the shame they threw at God to come back on their own heads. This is where Malachi lands in 2:9, because this whole disputation concerns the honour of God's name. The question is, what is God going to do about this travesty? Malachi 2:1–2 tells us: God is going to send a 'curse'. Indeed, we discover that he has already been cursing them. But what is this curse that Malachi is talking about?

The role of the priests in the Old Testament was to mediate between God and the people and to lead the people. Every day the priests would pronounce the Aaronic blessing of Numbers 6:24–26: 'The LORD bless you and keep you; the LORD make his face to shine upon you and be gracious to you; the LORD lift up his countenance upon you and give you peace.' Whenever Jews thought about the priests, probably those words would spring to mind in the first instance. Whilst it is hard to see in our English translations, it is clear from the Hebrew that Malachi deliberately uses many of the words from this 'Aaronic blessing'.

Malachi 2:2 tells us that these blessings which the priests gave repeatedly every day would be ineffectual and, further, would bring trouble to Israel instead of blessing. That is because their sin was not forgiven. The priests whose very job it was to offer sacrifices, to seek forgiveness and to bless God's people would find that their sacrifices were not accepted and so they could not bless others with forgiveness; they could only curse. In a sense, this was a reversal of Balaam's problem. He was hired to curse God's people, but each time, when he came to it, he could only bless them (Num. 22–24). Here, the priests of God were meant to bless God's people, but all they could do was curse.

The priests had made many sacrifices at particular feast days, but God had rejected their sacrifices. They remained unforgiven. When a sacrifice was made, the offal of the animal would be removed and taken outside the camp, because it was designated 'unclean'. In Malachi 2:3, certainly God is rejecting their sacrifices, but he is doing something far worse. The word translated 'dung' is actually the word for 'offal': God is saying that the unclean offal, or dung, of the sacrifice will be wiped across their faces. These sacrifices were not making anyone clean; quite the reverse. The uncleanness of the sacrifices would cover even the faces of the priests. In other words, the priests would be just like the offal. They would be removed from God's people and taken outside the camp.

This is a shocking image. The priests were meant to be holy, set apart for God. They were meant to be highly honoured. But now they would have dung over their faces and would be banished from the camp. Their shame could not be greater.

The result of unacceptable worship is deep shame—something I'm sure we all want to avoid. So how are we to come to God? What is the route to acceptable worship?

The route to acceptable worship (1:6, 14; 2:4–7)

To answer this question, we need to work out why God is highlighting the terrible results of their unacceptable worship. As we seek to understand the heart of God in Malachi, Leviticus 26 helps. The first third of that chapter describes the blessing that comes when God's people keep the covenant. The remainder of the chapter concerns the curses which will come when God's people break the covenant. The major help in understanding the heart of God is found in the use of the little word 'if' in those latter two-thirds of the chapter:

> But *if* you will not listen to me . . . *if* you spurn my statutes, and *if* your soul abhors my rules, so that you will not do all my commandments, but break my covenant, then I will do this to you: I will visit you with panic, with wasting disease and fever that consume the eyes and make the heart ache . . . And *if* in spite of this you will not listen to me, then I will discipline you again sevenfold for your sins . . . Then *if* you walk contrary to me and will not listen to me, I will continue striking you, sevenfold for your sins. And I will let loose the wild beasts against you, which shall bereave you of your children and destroy your livestock and make you few in number . . . And *if* by this discipline you are not turned to me but walk contrary to me, then I also will walk contrary to you, and I myself will strike you sevenfold for your sins . . . (Lev. 26:14–24)

In other words, the purpose of God's discipline is that people might return to God and serve him again. We notice the same idea in Malachi 2:2: '*If* you will not listen . . . ' Why is God telling them all this through Malachi? Because he wants their repentance and trust. He wants them to return to him and serve him as they should.

The covenant is central here—2:4b–5a is clear on that. God wants a relationship with his people. As far as God is concerned, the covenant brings 'life and peace' for his people (2:5) *in order that* we revere him and stand in awe of his name. It is the honour of God that is paramount. As this paragraph unfolds we discover the results of keeping covenant. The one who keeps covenant speaks 'true instruction', walks with God 'in peace and uprightness' and turns many from sin (2:6). I don't know about you, but for me, that's something to strive for!

In the Abrahamic covenant God's people were promised, 'I will make your descendants as the sand on the seashore.' But in Malachi 2:3, we have a phrase that probably means 'I will diminish your descendants'. In other words, the curse Malachi is proclaiming here is to do with reducing their offspring. This is a direct reversal of the covenant. To reverse their blessing was a direct response to their breaking of the covenant. God is telling them that the covenant blessings will no longer be theirs.

Now look at 2:4–5, where Malachi talks about a covenant of 'peace'. I am persuaded that this refers back to Numbers 25:12. In that chapter, it seems that God's people (the men in particular) were indulging in deep sin. Horribly, they were engaging in prostitution in broad daylight. As a result, God's anger burned against them and a plague broke out. In the midst of this came Phinehas, grandson of Aaron (and therefore a Levite, Exod. 6:25), who saw a man take a Midianite woman into his tent in the middle of the day. Phinehas was so angry that God's name was being dishonoured in this way that he rushed into the tent and drove his spear through both of them, killing them. Because of his zeal for the honour of God, God's anger was turned aside and the plague stopped. Numbers 25:11–12 reads, 'Phinehas son of Eleazar, the son of Aaron, the priest, has turned my anger away from the Israelites. Since he was as zealous for my honour among them as I am . . . I am making my covenant of peace with him' (NIV).

Earlier, when Moses was up the mountain receiving the law from God, the Israelites decided to bow in worship to a golden calf. God was incensed. But there in Exodus 32 it was the Levites who had zeal for God's name and killed the three thousand people who had led the idolatry. That was true zeal for God's name. In Malachi 1:10, God laments that there is not one leader willing to shut the doors of the sanctuary, to stop these pretend sacrifices from being made. No one will stand up and lead. No one has zeal for the name of God.

The point is that leaders must lead with real zeal. They must love God wholeheartedly. They must be willing to stand against what is wrong for the glory of Jesus, even when standing that way is hard. Sometimes, leaders must take drastic measures for the sake of God's name. They are called to have real zeal for him.

Before we get carried away, though, we're not meant to kill people off today because they have gone against God! In the time of Moses, the people of God were a theocracy under God's direct rule. This is not true today; we live in very different circumstances, wherever we live in the world, under the authority of men and women, most of whom are not Christians. We must not translate what happened with ancient Israel into how things should be in our nations today. The people of God in the Old Testament are in a similar position to the church of today, with the obvious rider that the church is not a nation state with civil and judicial laws, but rather is made up of God's people voluntarily committed one to another under the authority of its co-equal leaders. Zeal for the Lord in our churches will not involve killing off people who don't toe the line! Indeed, we must love people deeply, because zeal expressed without love is not godly zeal at all. The point of Malachi is that the grounds for God's discipline of his people is his love for them. As we have noted before, the purpose of his discipline is to elicit repentance. This is always how it should be. Zealous leaders must lead from a heart of godly love, being open themselves to correction and discipline. The actions of Phinehas in Numbers 25 and of the Levites in Exodus 32 may have been hard, but they were also open and honest. Nothing was done behind closed doors: godly zeal was in action openly, for all to see. Perhaps zeal should always be expressed openly and honestly. In fact, at root, secrecy is satanic.

As we think and pray about the appointment of leaders, we must ask this question: Are they zealous for the glory of God and the honouring of his name? God punishes in order to purify. He wants the covenant with Levi to continue, so he must admonish. Levi was zealous for God's name, and here in 2:4–6 Malachi holds Levi up as one to be honoured because he took his responsibilities seriously. His zeal was a godly zeal—open, honest and strong.

The responsibilities of the priesthood in the Old Testament are outlined in 2:6–7. The priests were to be truthful and accurate in instructing people in God's word. They were to be morally upright and to follow the Lord closely themselves. And they were to seek to turn people from their sin to God (this is both evangelism and discipleship). What Levi had done in Moses' day, the priests were meant to do in Malachi's day; there was to be no shadow of turning to the right or to the left.

Just as the priests in the Old Testament were to lead God's people, so the leaders in our churches today must seek to do likewise. The role of our leaders is the same: (a) to learn God's Word deeply; (b) to live upright lives determinedly; and (c) to lead by example to love God devotedly. If we're considering appointing leaders, perhaps these three things should be uppermost in our minds. Do they learn God's word deeply? Do they live upright lives determinedly? Do they lead by example to love God devotedly?

As we have noted, Levi is held up as an example for the priests in Malachi's day. In Malachi 2:7, Malachi tells us that a priest is a messenger of the Lord Almighty. In part, this is a reference back to Malachi himself, whose name means messenger of God (1:1). But it is also a reference forward to Jesus himself, our great High Priest, who has come for us. What did he do? People sought to learn from him, he spoke truth, he walked with God in peace and uprightness, and he turned many from sin. How did he achieve this? By his giving up his life. The one towards whom all the Old Testament sacrifices pointed, and to whom the commitment of Levi pointed, now has come—not *a* but *the* messenger of the Lord Almighty (2:7). He set his heart to honour his Father. This priest *was* perfect, and he offered himself freely and with abundant generosity (2:6). True instruction was in his mouth and nothing false was found on his lips. He walked with God in righteousness and peace. In fact, he was the Prince of peace. And he turned many from their sin.

In 1 Peter 2:5 and 9, Peter writes,

> You also, like living stones, are being built into a spiritual house to be a holy priesthood, offering spiritual sacrifices acceptable to God through Jesus Christ . . . You are a chosen people, a royal priesthood, a holy nation, God's special possession, that you may declare the praises of him who called you out of darkness into his wonderful light. (NIV)

There are still some in God's family who are especially to be set apart for ministry, and this is right, following the pattern of Acts 2. However, more broadly, all of God's people are priests. Collectively, we are 'a royal priesthood'. This means that all of us are to learn God's Word deeply, live upright lives determinedly, and lead people to love God devotedly. We are to do this for one primary reason: the honour of his name.

If we fail to do this, we can expect Jesus to be ashamed of us on that final day. If we're not truly submitted to Jesus, we're not part of God's family in a true sense. We may be *in* church, but we're not *part of* God's church. If that is the case for us, Malachi is warning, we are in danger of hearing the words, 'I never knew you.'

So how are we to worship God acceptably? The answer is found right here in 1:6 and 1:14: the route to right worship is right relationship. God describes himself as Father, Master and King. This means that, if we are his people, we are his sons,[3] his servants and his subjects. So we should live that way! These truths should lead us to love and to obey, two sides of the same coin. As far as relationship with God is concerned, if a person does not obey, they do not love.

So as we consider the sacrifices we make, let's make them in the light of honouring our majestic God. If truly he is our Master, our Father and our King, our sacrifices will seem small in the light of his sacrifice. If you are a leader of a church: Do you strive for your best? Do you correctly handle the word of truth? And for all of us: Do we test everything against the

Scriptures, as the Bereans did? Note that this doesn't apply only to the sermon, although it does apply to that. It applies also to the songs, the corporate prayers and the way the service is put together. It applies to the putting out of the chairs or how we conduct ourselves on the welcome team; how we do the church cleaning; or our approach to making the refreshments, doing the flowers or teaching the Sunday school. Why do we do these things? To show willing? So people notice we're doing something? So that we can say that we give something? Or do we serve in order to worship and serve the Lord?

I find these questions hard, but we *must* ask them of ourselves. Is God truly my Master, my Father and my King?

This is not a message to try harder, though we must. It is a message to love Jesus more, to recognize him for who he is, to ask for his work in us to change us for his glory. We want to offer acceptable sacrifices to God, because he is holy.

As we saw at the beginning, similar questions can be asked of us in terms of our lives outside the church building, too. We should ask ourselves questions about our approach to school, college, university, the workplace, home, family, university, shopping, hobbies, sports, music—in fact, life in its entirety.

We must ask these questions because, wherever you work, whatever you do, paid or unpaid, wherever you are: if you're a Christian, you carry the name of Jesus. You are saying to those around, 'This is how followers of Jesus work. This is how we live in the light of all he has done for us. This is how we speak to people around us. This is how much we care for others. This is how much worth we give to the Lord.'

How far short of this ideal we fall! How much we desire to live this way, and yet repeatedly offer unacceptable worship! I, for one, often echo the words of Paul in Romans 7: 'I do not do the good I want, but the evil I do not want is what I keep on doing' (Rom. 7:19). I am comforted that even the apostle Paul struggled with sin and with not living God's way.

Thankfully, the message here in Malachi is not 'try harder'. Such a message would be damning: we cannot offer acceptable worship *to* God without the indwelling help *of* God. Malachi is not driving us towards legalism. Neither is any other text in Scripture. Instead, Malachi is urging us to remember the gospel. 'Recognize how fallen you are,' he urges. Why? Because seeing our brokenness drives us to our Saviour, who was broken on our behalf. Our sin pushes us to the cross.

The heart of the gospel is that the innocent (Jesus) died on behalf of the guilty (us). Indeed, just as Abel (righteous) was killed by Cain (unrighteous), so the righteous Jesus was put to death by unrighteous people. But Jesus was no helpless victim. He could have called upon twelve legions of angels (Matt. 26:53). Indeed, he could simply have cried out, 'Enough!' and that would have been that. The power Jesus displayed at the crucifixion was not weak because he *couldn't* come down from the cross, but strong because he *didn't* come down from the cross. He saw his punishment right to the end—right to when he cried, 'It is finished!'

The work of dealing with our sin—yours (if you are a Christian) and mine—was completed. That included not only our past sin, but our present and future sin, too. Obviously, for Jesus all of our sin was future, and yet he dealt with it on the cross. Paul was not concerned that his current struggle against sin called into question his salvation; Jesus had died for him already. We should not be concerned either. It is not our salvation that is in question; it is our sanctification. So Malachi urges that we remember the gospel and so grow to love Jesus more, recognizing him for who he is, and asking for his work in us to change us for his glory.

If you are regularly in church but are not a Christian, why not submit to Jesus now? Don't let another day go by, lest you be for ever outside his kingdom, humiliated and shamed. Put aside your unacceptable sacrifices and submit your whole self to Jesus, the one who made the only truly acceptable sacrifice of himself to God on your behalf.

The ultimate purpose of this wonderful gospel, though, is not our salvation, although that is God's wonderful provision for us. Underneath everything else, the purpose of the gospel is God-centred, not man-centred. The prime reason why Jesus came was not just to save us, but to glorify God. He is the Lord of hosts, a name repeated over and over again in these verses. And to him alone belong praise, glory, honour . . . and worship. It is all about *him*!

Notes

1 B. B. Warfield, 'The Oracles of God' in *The Inspiration and Authority of the Bible*, ed. Samuel G. Craig (London: Marshall, Morgan & Scott, 1969), p. 403.

2 Of course, many Far and Near Eastern cultures today are also built around shame and honour. The 'guilt' culture I describe is more Western, although perhaps growing in prevalence.

3 In ancient Near Eastern culture, it was the sons who inherited; daughters did not. Therefore, the people of God—male and female—are often referred to as 'sons', not because the Bible is sexist, but rather to ensure that women know they are included in the inheritance. Women have to get used to the idea of being 'sons of God' just as men have to get used to the idea of being part of the Bride of Christ.

Faithlessness v. faithfulness: the person of God (2:10–16)

W hen I was younger, I remember learning that arch bridges are built of carefully shaped stones, with each one resting on those beneath. Every arch bridge has a 'keystone'—the stone in the middle at the top. As a load crosses the bridge, the weight is distributed via the keystone to each stone beneath it. The stones are shaped in such a way that no stone can fall unless the ones beneath fall first, and the integrity of the whole structure depends upon this keystone. Everything runs up to it, and everything runs down from it.

There is a similar structure commonly found in Hebrew and Greek literature. A paragraph, chapter or even an entire book in Hebrew will often have an arch-like structure. The text is written in such a way that the pattern running through it is, for example, A to B to C, back to B and then back to A. Partly, this pattern was used as a mnemonic device: it helped people to remember what was written. But the pattern was also used for another reason: it drew attention to the keystone, the centre point of the pattern. Each pair of 'bricks' builds on the ones beneath them, and they build up to the keystone—the crux of the matter—right there in the middle.

When I first came across it, I found this pattern quite foreign to my Western way of thinking. I had learned that we should think chronologically and progressively. For many of us, the climax of an argument is usually at the end. But ancient classical writers sometimes liked to put the focus in the middle of a piece of writing rather than at the end, so they structured their texts in this arch-like pattern to draw attention to the mid-point.[1] More formally, this pattern is known as a 'chiasm' (or 'chiasmus') and the structure may be described as 'chiastic', from the cross-shaped Greek letter X ('Chi').

The structure of Malachi's third disputation

As we turn to the third disputation in Malachi 2:10–16, we find a great example of this 'chiastic' structure in an ABCBA pattern. We do not see it quite so easily in our English translations, but it is present nonetheless. Here it is, laid out to emphasize the structure:

A [10] Have we not all one Father? Has not one God created us? Why then are we faithless to one another, profaning the covenant of our fathers?

B [11] Judah has been faithless, and abomination has been committed in Israel and in Jerusalem. For Judah has profaned the sanctuary of the LORD, which he loves, and has married the daughter of a foreign god. [12] May the LORD cut off from the tents of Jacob any descendant of the man who does this, who brings an offering to the LORD of hosts!

C [13] And this second thing you do. You cover the LORD's altar with tears, with weeping and groaning because he no longer regards the offering or accepts it with favour from your hand.

B' [14] But you say, 'Why does he not?' Because the LORD was witness between you and the wife of your youth, to whom you have been faithless, though she is your companion and your wife by covenant. [15] Did he not make them one, with a portion of the Spirit in their union? And what was the one God seeking? Godly offspring. So guard yourselves in your spirit, and let none of you be faithless to the wife of your youth. [16] 'For the man who does not love his wife but divorces her, says the LORD, the God of Israel, covers his garment with violence, says the LORD of hosts.

A' So guard yourselves in your spirit, and do not be faithless.'

Both verse 10 and verse 16 begin with two lines of Hebrew poetry. Both those verses end with comments about breaking faith: 'Why are we faithless?' and 'do not be faithless'. So the 'A' part of the chiasm concerns the abhorrence of faithlessness.

Verse 11 begins with this same idea: 'Judah has been faithless', and verse 14 includes 'to [her] you have been faithless' as well. Verse 12 says, 'May the LORD cut off from the tents of Jacob', and in verse 16 we again find this idea of cutting off and division, with the concept of divorce. Verses 11 and 12 concern interfaith marriage, whilst verses 14–16a concern divorce, both examples of faithlessness in close human relationships. These verses form part 'B' of the chiasm.

Finally, the keystone of the arch is verse 13, and this verse concerns a broken relationship with God: 'And this second thing you do. You cover the LORD's altar with tears, with weeping and groaning because he no longer regards the offering or accepts it with favour from your hand.' The crux of the matter is that there is something very wrong with their vertical relationship: the central relationship between them and God. This forms the 'C' at the centre of the chiasm.

So we can say that this structure gives us two examples of faithlessness in close human relationships, which both reflect and bracket the main problem: faithlessness in their relationship with God. God's call to his people through this third disputation is that they must start being faithful once more. As one who often strays from faithfulness to God, I need to hear these words as well.

Perhaps a good way to approach this chiasm is simply to follow its sequence. At each stage we'll come back to the centre point, because that is the focus of Malachi's message.

The abhorrence of faithlessness (2:10, 16b)

The poetry of verse 10 reads literally, 'Not Father one, have we? Not God one, has created us?' Unless you are fluent in yoda (!),[2] a re-ordering of the words improves the English translation: 'Have we not all one Father? Has not one God created us?' In other words, we are one family, with Creator God as our Father.

Malachi starts this way because the issue he's tackling concerns a major disconnection. People in the same family should be together and should be seeking to uphold the honour and good name of the family—that's basic shame-and-honour culture. Malachi's logic is simple: as we are meant to be one family, why do we profane the covenant of our fathers by breaking faith with one another? How can we claim to be God's covenant people on the one hand, and then deliberately and flagrantly break that covenant on the other? How can we claim to be in God's family and at the same time break faith with that family?

A covenant was a mutual and to-the-death commitment agreed between people. I think the covenant Malachi is eyeballing here is not the covenant of peace he mentioned a few verses back in 2:5, but rather the covenant central to God's plan throughout redemptive history. That central covenant was a binding agreement that God had made with his people in which he promised to be their God and that they would be his people. It was an agreement in which God promised to make a vast family of believers, provide them with a realm in which to rule, and through them reach out to others across the world. This was an agreement between Almighty God and his created people in which God committed himself to them. By the time of Malachi, God had remained faithful to that covenant for nigh on two thousand years.

For me, when temptation arises, it is sometimes helpful to remind myself of my covenant relationship with God and with other believers. To give into temptation is to break covenant, and doing that brings shame and dishonour, not just on me, but also upon others and, most importantly, on God himself. To put it another way, since the message of the gospel concerns the route by which God redeemed us and reaffirms his covenant, when temptation arises we need to fall on our knees before the cross, because Jesus *has* delivered us (past tense) from evil's clutches. If we are Christians, we are no longer chained to sin: the covenant is re-established; Jesus has broken the chains. Now we are chained to him, bound with his love, and free to resist and overcome temptation. I am part of God's family, so how can I even think of bringing him dishonour by giving into temptation?

In these verses, Malachi is pointing out that this wonderful covenant between God and his people is being flagrantly disregarded by God's people. Their faithlessness is abhorrent to God—so much so that, despite their weeping and wailing at the Lord's altar, God pays no attention to their offerings and does not accept them. Faithlessness is abhorrent to God. Refusing to submit to God is abhorrent to God. Refusing to live in the light of God's covenant is abhorrent to God. Living for self and disregarding God is abhorrent to God. Messy personal relationships are abhorrent to God.

Breaking faith (2:11–12, 14–16a)

Interfaith marriages (2:11–12)

Having contemplated the 'outer brackets' of the chiasm (the 'A' part, the 'bottom of the arch'), we come next to the bricks above them—part 'B' of the chiasm. These two bricks comprise two ways in which the people are breaking faith, both involving bad marriage practice. The first, here in 2:11–12, concerns 'interfaith marriage'.

Notice that in 2:11 Malachi describes the behaviour of the people of God as 'marr[ying] the daughter of a foreign god'. The men of Judah could be referred to as the 'sons of the true God', so, in a similar way, women outside the people of God (i.e. from foreign nations who worshipped foreign gods) could be described as 'daughters of a foreign god'. God's people were meant to trust in and follow the true God, and in law they were only allowed to be joined in marriage to those who were also part of God's people (i.e. 'daughters of the true God'). But in Malachi's day, the men were marrying foreign women—women who trusted in different gods, whatever those gods might be.

To be clear, the prohibition against interfaith marriage is not a prohibition against inter-racial or inter-ethnic marriage. Indeed, inter-racial and inter-ethnic marriages can honour God greatly, and there are some excellent examples within Scripture itself (e.g. between Boaz, an upright Jew, and Ruth the Moabitess). Instead, this prohibition of interfaith marriage is against marriage between one person who is a follower of God and another person who is not. In Malachi's day, God's people had broken faith by marrying those from other religions—those from the nations around them who worshipped and served foreign gods. These interfaith marriages were so commonplace that Malachi highlighted them as characteristic of the entire nation.

Through Malachi God uses extremely strong language to condemn such interfaith marriage: he says it is an 'abomination'. Perhaps one reason why his language is so strong is because God commanded them *not* to intermarry with foreign nations. Moses had written very clearly in Deuteronomy 7, 'Do not intermarry with them. Do not give your daughters to their sons or take their daughters for your sons' (Deut. 7:3 NIV). To marry someone from a foreign nation was to disobey God's direct order. Further, Moses gave a reason for this stipulation in the following verse: 'for they will turn your children away from following me to serve other gods, and the LORD's anger will burn against you' (v. 4 NIV).

The reason for God's dire warning against interfaith marriage was to save his people from spiritual disaster. The nations around Israel were idolaters, and so joining with them in marriage unions would, almost inevitably, result in people turning away from the one true God in order to indulge in idolatry as well. As in Moses' day, so in Malachi's day. Many of Malachi's contemporaries had married into different religions and, as a result, were now being drawn away from loving and serving the one true God.

And as in Malachi's day, so in Paul's day. Paul writes in 2 Corinthians 6:14, 'Do not be yoked together with unbelievers. For what do righteousness and wickedness have in common? Or what fellowship can light have with darkness?' (NIV). Such unions will almost inevitably result in the follower of God being drawn away.

And as in Paul's day, so in our day. A Christian, if they marry, must marry another Christian. They must not marry an unbeliever, or they will be drawn away from God. We see this happening in our Western world. There are believers who have married unbelievers and have been drawn away from trusting in the Lord Jesus. Other believers who have married unbelievers have found their marriages extremely difficult, and those marriages have been a source of sadness. I know of no such interfaith marriage where the Christian does not ache for their spouse to come to faith. For some of them, that event has still not occurred forty, fifty or sixty years after the marriage began. It simply does not make sense to wed yourself to one whose most fundamental drive lies in the opposite direction from your own.

Logically, this prohibition against interfaith marriage applies also to 'dating' relationships. If you are a Christian, you should never date someone who is not also a Christian. In my work with teenagers and young people, I have often heard Christian young men say, 'It's OK— she's interested in God. I think she'll come to faith soon.' And yet, inevitably, she does not, and the young man fades in his faith. Or a girl might say, 'It's not going to change my faith in the Lord just because he's not interested yet. I will remain strong!' And yet, some weeks, months or years later, that girl has stopped trusting in Jesus and no longer follows him at all. The fire dies down because a person has formed a close relationship with someone currently cold towards God. As Paul wrote,

'What do righteousness and wickedness have in common?' (2 Cor. 6:14 NIV). In the final analysis, the answer is, 'Not very much at all!'

It's easy to fall into the trap of thinking, 'It won't be that way for *me*,' but that is foolish. If we disobey God's clear instructions, it *will* be that way for us. If a hot coal spends a long time with a cold stone, the hot coal will get colder, and, before long, both will be lukewarm and God will spit them out of his mouth, as he puts it in Revelation 3:16. If you are a true believer in Jesus, contemplating sharing your life with someone whose heart passion runs counter to your own is courting disaster. Don't do it. And if you are dating an unbeliever, choose this day whom you will serve (Josh. 24:15). If you're going out with someone who is not a believer, stop it. Yes, it will hurt now, but if you do not stop it now, it will hurt far more later. Far better to remove the splinter than ignore it and allow infection to set in and fester.

We must feel the force of Malachi's pronouncement upon those who are unrepentantly married to unbelievers: 'May the LORD cut off from the tents of Jacob any descendant of the man who does this, who brings an offering to the LORD of hosts!' (Mal. 2:12). Even though this man brings his offerings to the temple, Malachi says, nonetheless he will be cut off because of his rebellion against God's specific command regarding interfaith marriage. That is how seriously God treats his command against a union between a believer and an unbeliever.

It is interesting to notice that God chooses to call his people by the name Judah rather than Israel or Jacob. I think this is primarily because Judah formed the line of kings (a line from which Jesus himself would be descended). Malachi 1:14 tells us that God is their King, and 2:10 tells us that God is their Father. If the king is your father, you are a prince or a princess. So Malachi calls them Judah to remind them that they are in God's royal family. This means both that they are highly privileged and that they have serious obligations to promote honour and to avoid bringing shame.

But despite this huge privilege and these great obligations, Judah has broken faith ('been faithless'). Is it any wonder Malachi moves on by using the word 'abomination'? An abomination has been committed, says Malachi. Although they are royal princes, due to inherit under God their King, they have married the daughters of a foreign god, bringing deep shame upon their family and upon their Father, the King.

In a similar way, if you have had the great privilege of being brought up in a Christian family, or brought up in the church (hopefully both!), but have failed to submit to Jesus and live for him, you have broken faith, which is an abomination; it is detestable in God's eyes. To be amongst God's covenant people on a regular basis is a huge privilege, one which we reject at our peril.

It someone has never heard of Jesus and never had the gospel explained to them, their rejection of God and even their following of idols is perhaps understandable. But to hear the gospel of Jesus at home and at church on a regular basis, to receive good Bible teaching, and yet still to refuse to submit to the One you *know* gave his life for you is an abomination to God.

The people in Malachi's day seemed to view the words of Moses as a quaint ancient document which shouldn't be taken too seriously and certainly wasn't applicable to their 'modern age'. How horribly familiar. We are surrounded by a society that takes the same view of God's Word. But we *must* take God's Word seriously, because he is God and he does not change, and neither does his Word. Interfaith marriage is an abhorrence to God.

God's strong words against interfaith marriage bring some obvious questions to mind for us today. If you are a Christian and you are married to an unbelieving wife or husband, what should you do? The deed is done, and this is the situation in which you find yourself. So what are you to do now? Let's address a few different situations.

- It may be that this situation has arisen because you were both unbelievers when you got married. Then you came to faith, but your husband or wife has not come to faith yet. What does this text say to you? Nothing. This text concerns people already in the church who choose to disobey God and marry unbelievers. It says nothing about those who were not Christians when they married unbelievers and who have since come to trust in Jesus. If this is your situation, then, as a follower of Jesus, your role is to pray regularly for your spouse and never to give up; and the role of other Christians is to pray with you and for you. After all, your spouse is your prime missionary responsibility. As Paul writes in 1 Corinthians 7:15–16, 'God has called you to peace. For how do you know, wife, whether you will save your husband? Or how do you know, husband, whether you will save your wife?'

- It may be, though, that as a Christian you chose to marry an unbelieving husband or wife despite the explicit command of God. This part of Malachi has much to say to you.

  » First of all, this passage is clear that you were wrong to marry in such circumstances. You did not take God's Word seriously enough. You thought you knew better. You let your own decision usurp the will of Almighty God. This passage is, then, a call to come in repentance to God.

  » Second, the Bible as a whole is clear that there is forgiveness available. No sin is beyond the reach of the cross. As you come to God in genuine repentance, you will find forgiveness, life, peace and rest for your soul. And if you have asked for forgiveness for this sin in the past, you stand forgiven. Do not allow the devil to make you feel guilty all over again.

  » Third, work hard to grow your love for Jesus each day. Whatever the day holds for you and your spouse, work hard to love Jesus more. You will need to work extra hard so that the fire doesn't burn low. Seek good Christian friends who will pray with you and for you and your spouse. And remember 1 Corinthians 7.

- Perhaps, though, you thought you were marrying a fellow believer—or did marry a fellow believer—but your spouse has since walked away from the Lord and perhaps also from the marriage. Where does that leave you, as one seeking to follow the Lord? Again, Malachi 2 does not speak into your situation. What is clear from Scripture more broadly is that your role, as for every Christian, is to seek to love Jesus more each day. God is still your King and your Father, and his deep and passionate love for you remains unchanged.

Whatever heartache may be ours, we must remember that, in the final analysis, human marriage is a picture of something far greater and far more dependable: the final marriage between Jesus and his bride, the church (as we will see below). This is the underlying reason why interfaith marriage is abhorrent to God. Marriage is meant to depict that final perfect marriage, but interfaith marriage can never do that. Interfaith marriage could never depict aright that perfect marriage in which there is no danger of divorce, infidelity, secrecy, misunderstandings, pet hates, irritations, money stresses, abuse or anything else contrary to God's perfection. Right marriage should involve two lovers of God growing towards the True Bridegroom as they grow together—a marriage of three persons, we could say. Only in right marriage can such a picture emerge.

In-the-faith divorce (2:14–16a)

But Malachi also gives us a second example of breaking faith on the other side of the chiasm—something I have termed 'in-the-faith' divorce. To marry someone who is an unbeliever is to be in danger of syncretism, of being led astray to follow other gods, of allowing the fire of faith to grow cold under constant attack from the human being closest to us. It is a very dangerous road to walk. But the second way of breaking faith which

Malachi describes here is even worse. To divorce someone who is a believer, to whom one has been committed and with whom one has walked the road to heaven, is to strike fair and square against God.

In Malachi 2:14 Malachi is loud and clear: 'you have been faithless' to 'the wife of your youth'. For whatever reason, people in Malachi's day had divorced their wives. If you are a married man: have you been faithless to the wife of your youth? Have you had a secret affair of which you continue to know the shame? Have you had numerous affairs through pornography? Have you committed adultery in your imagination? Malachi's heartfelt hope is that we might come even now in repentance, seek forgiveness and plead for reconciliation. It is time to stand, committed to our wives, faithful and willing to lead. Likewise, married women are called to be committed to their husbands, faithful and true. If you are married, you have made a covenant with your spouse in the sight of Almighty God. Do not be faithless to them, because that is abhorrent to God.

Malachi reiterates: if you are a husband, the wife of your youth is your companion and your wife by covenant. Think for a moment of the commitment: 'For better, for worse; for richer, for poorer, in sickness and in health, till death do us part.' Marriage is a very serious thing and never to be taken lightly. Further, it is never to be annulled lightly. 'Be faithful to your wife' is Malachi's cry here.

It is helpful to understand the way in which Jewish marriages worked in first-century Palestine. Whilst there is significant variation in the historical record, it seems that there were essentially seven main steps:

1. The father (it was almost always the father of the family) arranged for his son to be married and the woman whom his son was to marry. He would arrange this with the father (and family) of the bride, sometimes without the input of the intended bride, and often when the bride and groom were very young.[3]

2. The father of the bridegroom would pay a considerable sum (a *mohar*) to purchase the bride.

3. The man and the woman were betrothed. The betrothal was a solemn agreement, rather like a very serious engagement. To break a betrothal required a certificate of divorce, and was a rare occurrence.

4. Then the man would return home to his father's house and prepare a room, a bridal chamber, for his bride. He would take perhaps up to a year to prepare the perfect place for her in his father's house. During this time, he and his bride-to-be would not have face-to-face contact. He would not see her and she would not see him.

5. Once the groom was prepared, he would gather his household together and lead a joyful procession to the house of his bride. Trumpets would sound. Music would play. Shouts would proclaim his return.

6. At this point, the bride was expected to be ready. Although she didn't actually know when the bridegroom would come, she was expected to be ready to drop everything at the sound of the wedding trumpets and the marriage procession coming down the road. Then the groom would arrive, greet his wife-to-be and take her (and the wedding procession) back to his father's house, and to the special room he had prepared for her.

7. On arrival, all the guests were given special wedding garments to wear, the door was shut, and the ceremony and party began. As the party progressed, the bride and groom entered the bridal chamber and the marriage was consummated (in fact, someone was specifically assigned the task of announcing the consummation of the marriage to the gathered guests!). The wedding reception often went on for a whole week.[4]

Learning about these common wedding practices in the ancient Near East is very helpful for understanding a number of Bible passages, not least those concerning the return of Jesus. The bridegroom (Jesus) will return for his bride (the church) and take her to be with him in the place he has prepared.

As one example, consider Revelation 19:6–9:

> Hallelujah!
> For our Lord our God
>> the Almighty reigns.
> Let us rejoice and exult
>> and give him the glory,
> for the marriage of the Lamb [that's Jesus] has come,
>> and his Bride [that's the church] has made herself ready;
> it was granted her to clothe herself
>> with fine linen, bright and pure . . .
> 'Blessed are those who are invited to the marriage supper of the Lamb.'

Malachi has much to say about marriage and divorce. But even if you are not married, if you are a Christian, you *are* betrothed. This first-century Palestine approach to weddings is but a shadow of God's work for us:

- The Father has arranged for the marriage of his Son to his bride, the church.
- The price paid for the bride was huge: the death of the bridegroom, in fact.
- Jesus has given his life for us, and, if we're Christians, we have given ourselves to him. We could say that the betrothal has happened. If we are Christians, we are now united to Christ, but we are awaiting his return.
- Jesus has gone back to his Father's house to prepare a place for us there.
- One day, we will hear the trumpet sounds and the music and the joyful procession as Jesus returns with the angels of heaven.

- We do not know when Jesus will return, but we are expected to be ready, as Jesus often said.
- When Jesus arrives he will take us, his bride, to our eternal home in his Father's house.
- He will provide wedding garments for his bride, the doors will be shut, and then the party will begin.

This will be the greatest wedding party of all, far better than any wedding party you could ever have in this life (even better than my own wedding, which was awesome). This end-of-time wedding will be, quite literally, 'out of this world'. And eternal marriage bliss will follow it.

Malachi uses the phrase 'the wife of your youth' because marriages were often made between very young people. These were marriages made within the covenant community—between, supposedly, a man of God and a woman of God. Did you see how this disputation began with a reminder that God is their Father? He is the one who arranges marriages. He had it planned way before they ever did. So to divorce was to seek to annul the will of God; and yet they *were* divorcing. God had arranged their marriages, so they should remain faithful.

What if you are not married? Perhaps marriage is in the future for you. If so, remember that it is your Father in heaven who arranges marriages. Your role is not to 'go fishing', but to find all your fulfilment and satisfaction in Jesus. As you wait, you can focus on growing to know Jesus better and better, serving him more and more, and becoming the best husband or wife material you can be.

Or perhaps you were once married but now are widowed or divorced. Or perhaps you're not married because the Lord has entirely different plans for you. Perhaps the Lord needs you at the moment for a particular committed ministry you could not do if you were married.

Perhaps God needs you simply to display to a sexually addicted culture that fidelity and virginity need not detract from joy and fulfilment—indeed, joy, satisfaction, fulfilment and wonder are far above the momentary pleasures of sex. Only single people can display that fact with crystal clarity. Or perhaps you struggle with same-sex attraction, and so the Lord calls you to demonstrate, like Job, that love for, commitment to and obedience to the Lord need not depend on circumstances or personal struggles. Rather, obedience to the Lord in your life is a powerful testimony in a way it could never be in the lives of others who don't have those struggles. A commitment from a Christian who has same-sex attraction to live a life of fidelity and abstinence is a beautiful thing that humbles me. How we must pray for people of faith who fight the flesh for the glory of God! 'Well done, my good and faithful servant!' will be shouted from the rooftops when such people get to glory.

For some, your role is to encourage and strengthen those marriages around you as much as you are able, and also to encourage and strengthen the unmarried around you as much as you are able. They need your prayers, love and guidance.

For some, divorce has intervened and this is an area of much pain and difficulty—self-blame, perhaps, or suffering at the hands of another. Perhaps there is shame, too. But you, maybe more than any other, know how to love, support and befriend those with serious marital problems, or those more recently divorced, because you understand from the inside some of that pain, that sense of betrayal, that same suffering. Perhaps you even know what it means to suffer at the hands of the one who was meant to love and cherish you. What vital, practical ministry needs to happen right here! And you are best placed to offer it if you have walked that road yourself.

Finally, in this section, we come to Malachi 2:15–16a. The Hebrew of the first half of verse 15 is very problematic. One commentator described it as the most difficult verse in the whole of the Old Testament. It seems that no one really knows either what it says or what it means. Nevertheless, Bible translators baulk at the idea of getting to the end of verse 14 and then writing, 'No idea how to translate this part, so we'll move on to the next bit, which is clearer!'

Verse 16 is problematic, too. The NIV 1984 translated it: '"I hate divorce," says the LORD God of Israel, "and I hate a man's covering himself with violence as well as with his garment," says the LORD Almighty.' But there is now a general consensus amongst more recent commentators that this is not the way to translate the Hebrew. A better translation might be '"He who hates and divorces [implied: 'the wife of his youth'}," says the LORD God of Israel, "covers his garment with violence," says the LORD of hosts.'

So it seems to me that verses 15 and 16 have a 'compare and contrast' approach. Both end with, 'Guard yourselves in your spirit, and do not be faithless [to the wife of your youth].' Verse 15 is talking about oneness and unity; and verse 16 is talking about disunity and divorce. Perhaps the first verse says, 'Stay married, because your unity in marriage reflects God's design for unity. Do not be faithless in your marriage.' And perhaps the second verse then says, 'He who hates and divorces his wife does violence to them both, tearing apart the unity God designed for you. Do not be faithless in your marriage.'

What about 2:15a? What is it saying? To be honest, I am not sure. Further, perhaps it doesn't really matter! Whilst I do not understand the *reason* Malachi is giving, I *do* understand the instruction. Malachi 2:15 ends with the statement: 'Guard yourselves in your spirit, and let none of you be faithless to the wife of your youth.' So it seems that the first half of the verse forms an argument, or a *reason*, for the instruction. And even if we're not sure of the content of this reason, nevertheless the instruction is clear.

God made a covenant with Abraham, Isaac and Jacob, not with Abraham, Isaac and Esau. Esau is outside the covenant. He is hated by God because of his sin. This is the point Malachi makes in Malachi 1 and which Paul takes up in Romans 9. A man makes a covenant with the wife of his youth, to love and cherish her from the date of the marriage until death parts them. His wife is integral to the covenant. Here in Malachi, the man hates and divorces his wife, not because of anything in her, but because of his own sinful heart.

God hates a person who is outside the covenant because of that person's sinful heart. But this man hates another (his wife) who is inside the covenant because of his own sinful heart. And that is a terrible thing indeed.

What does it mean to say that he 'covers his garment with violence'? What is that violence? Perhaps it is the tearing apart of what God has joined together. Marriage, fundamentally, is of God and joins two people together deeply and spiritually. This joining can be expressed in sexual intimacy, but it goes much deeper than that. In divorcing the wife of his youth, a man is airing his dirty laundry in public—his garment is covered with violence. The union between the two is there, consummated sexually, but he is ripping it apart. Such divorce is abhorrent to God.

Here in Malachi, the central relationship the people are meant to have and cultivate is with God. But this relationship is absent.

Central relationship: from absent to actual (2:13)

We come at last to the keystone of the arch in verse 13. This keystone may surprise us. The central point is as simple as it is stark: sometimes God refuses to forgive.

The people in Malachi's day are weeping and wailing at God's altar, wanting his forgiveness and wanting him to pay attention. But God does not forgive them and neither does he pay any attention. Just as in 1:9–10 the people are asking God for forgiveness in a sinful way, so here the people are asking God to forgive them whilst they continue to live in rebellion against him.

They have no genuine desire to put things right or to live God's way. Neither are they sorrowful over their sinfulness or regretting their opposition to God. Rather they are just hoping that if they say the right words, they can continue to live sinfully, comfortable in the knowledge that God will forgive them. The have religiosity, perhaps, but they do not have true faith. And God will not forgive them.

Sometimes God refuses to forgive. This is true even if we cry, wail and make a show of wanting God's forgiveness. God sees the heart, and if the heart of a man or woman is not seeking to live in submission to him, but is continuing to live in rebellion, God will not forgive. Here in Malachi God is telling them that what should be their central relationship (the one with himself) is non-existent.

Interfaith marriages are abhorrent to God. In-the-faith divorces are also abhorrent to God. But why is this? Because, at root, every earthly marriage is meant to picture the coming marriage of Jesus with his church, which we discussed earlier. This perfect marriage is one in which there will be no disagreement. It is a marriage where there will be total unity, commitment and love. An interfaith marriage misses this supreme picture because it is, at root, a house divided against itself. One person is on the road to heaven, while the other is riding firmly in the opposite direction. One person is seeking to glorify Jesus; the other is ignoring him altogether, or worse. Marriage displays unity, but how can it do that with two people who have disunity at the core of their being?

In-the-faith divorce misses this supreme picture because it openly tears apart a covenant bond. It suggests that the final marriage between Christ and the church can be broken. This heavenly marriage is an eternal covenant which God has made with his people, a covenant which cannot be broken. In-the-faith divorce scores deep gashes across what is meant to be a beautiful picture of the most glorious marriage of all.[5]

The central point, the keystone of the arch, reminds us that the heart of the Christian faith concerns a right relationship between a person and his or her Creator. This relationship exists only when there is genuine repentance and submission on the human side of the relationship, because without our repentant heart and submission to God, there is no forgiveness.

For those who are married or are soon to be married, it's very helpful to remember the picture our marriages are meant to portray. God should be the first person in my marriage, because marriages are made in heaven.

A request for forgiveness is only genuine if we're committed to change. If we really want God's forgiveness, we'll 'guard [ourselves] in [our] spirit [in our hearts]' and will not break faith (Mal. 2:16b). We will live differently.

Notice that this is not a gospel of works. God is not saying, 'Unless you sort yourselves out, I won't forgive you.' If that were the message, none of us would have any hope, because we *can't* sort ourselves out. Getting our lives cleaned up is God's work within us as we strive to love him more; it is not our work that we do by ourselves.

But the gospel message is a betrothal offered by Jesus himself. He has given his life in order to pay for our sin and to offer us forgiveness. He has risen from death to prove his victory over sin and death. He has ascended into heaven, where he has gone to prepare for his bride a room—a bridal chamber. The gospel message, then, *is* a recognition of our failure, a genuine recognition of our need to be saved, forgiven and changed, and a heartfelt response to Jesus as Lord and King, ruling our lives from now on. If we have that central relationship with God in place, we are heading for eternity with our bridegroom, Jesus. Every Christian is part of God's universal church and will be in attendance at that great final wedding between Jesus, the bridegroom, and his bride—his people, the church.

It has often been said that we must keep the main thing the main thing. How are we to ensure that our relationship with God is front and centre? What practical steps can we take to this end?

The answers to this question revolve around the nature of relationships. How do we maintain a close relationship with anyone, whether a friend, spouse or family member? First, we spend time with them regularly.

Second, we keep short accounts—that is, we recognize when we get it wrong and seek forgiveness quickly. Third, we look for ways to bring the other person blessing. Fourth, we seek to support and encourage their family, too.

Our relationship with God is very similar, although the priorities may be in a slightly different order. First, as is clear from the keystone of the arch in this section of Malachi, we *must* keep short accounts. We must have genuine repentance before God; without that, there is no forgiveness at all and, consequently, no relationship at all. Turning from our waywardness and sin and turning towards the living Lord Jesus is the only way by which we may be saved. This is step 1 in the divine–human relationship. It is also the keynote of our ongoing relationship with him. We must return to the cross daily, keeping short accounts and seeking his forgiveness. If the cross is central, we will stay on course.

Following quickly on the heels of keeping short accounts comes the need to spend time with God regularly. Reading the Bible carefully and committedly and coming to God in prayer every day are vital for our relationship with God to flourish. We must fight for our daily time with Jesus. We must encourage one another to fight in this way, too.

Third, we must seek to support and encourage God's family, namely, other Christians. This brings God much blessing. Our circumstances will probably afford us much opportunity to bring blessing to others, whether through diligent prayer for them or through practical help or relational closeness in times of struggle.

Of course, there are some safeguards we can put in place to help buttress ourselves against falling into sin. 'Guard yourselves in your spirit,' Malachi writes (2:16): we are to put measures in place to help us stay faithful. For me, for example, I need to avoid difficult conversations when I am tired! Perhaps we should give financially a bit more than we are comfortable with, and check our giving regularly. Perhaps we need software on our electronic devices to restrict our viewing. Perhaps, if we have to stay a night away, we should get the hotel to send a copy of an itemized bill to our company or spouse, including our TV viewing. Maybe we should ask someone to commit to praying for us as we fight our anger. Keeping a log of our Bible reading may help us to keep it a priority.

Why must we guard ourselves? In order that we will 'not be faithless' (2:16). In Malachi's context, he is talking about faithfulness to the wife of one's youth. But in the broader context, the whole book concerns faithfulness to God. We are to guard ourselves in our spirit so that we will be faithful to him. We are to maintain our vertical relationship with God. In doing so, our horizontal relationships will be easier to navigate. As we stay faithful, we look forward to that great marriage supper of the Lamb. We await *his* glorious coming to take us finally to his and our eternal home which he, our bridegroom, has been preparing for us.

Notes

1 This pattern is sometimes described in other ways. For example, it can be seen as a concentric pattern, a bit like an archery target or darts board, constructed of concentric circles, one circle inside another, inside another.

2 In the *Star Wars* film series, Yoda is a character renowned for putting the verb or verbal phrase at the end of spoken sentences, e.g. 'When you look at the dark side, careful you must be' (*Star Wars: Episode III—Revenge of the Sith*, 2005).

3 Often marriages occurred when the bride and groom were still in their teens. This was likely the case for Mary and Joseph, who were probably betrothed whilst Mary was still a mid-teenager.

4 See Hayyim Schauss, 'Ancient Jewish Marriage', https://www.myjewishlearning.com/article/ancient-jewish-marriage/, accessed 10 January 2019.

5 Sometimes divorce needs to happen—perhaps necessary because of repeated marital unfaithfulness or domestic abuse. But divorce is never *good* because it undercuts the beauty of that eternal marriage which it is meant to mirror.

Sacred suffering: the agony of God (2:17–3:5)

D aytona Beach in Florida, USA, is a beautiful long, straight beach with gentle waves and miles of sand. My family are not really a 'beach' sort of family, but when we lived in the USA we loved going to Daytona as a way to cool off from the hot Florida sun, and it was only an hour's drive from our home. Occasionally, however, there are strong rip currents which can pull you out to sea. On one afternoon we realized that a man in the water had got into difficulties because of a dangerous rip tide. He was struggling hard against the current, floundering around, getting further from the shore and tiring himself out. Thankfully, the coastguard arrived promptly and dispatched a couple of lifeguards to rescue him. They grabbed a body-board and dived under the waves, swimming expertly and swiftly to get to the rapidly tiring man. When they reached him, they hauled him onto the board and pulled him across the rip current into calmer water. Then they swam back to shore, towing the man behind them.

The standard advice for someone caught in a rip tide is to swim across it to calmer water before swimming back to the shore. The swimmer's problem was that he was struggling against the current and was therefore unable to escape its grip. As we come to the fourth disputation in Malachi, we find that, like that swimmer at Daytona Beach, the people of God were struggling in the wrong way. And just like him, if they continued to struggle in the wrong way, it would lead to death.

When I face trials and suffering in life, I often do the same thing: I struggle the wrong way. I forget how I am meant to respond to them. So I need to learn again from Malachi: what is the right way to struggle?

We will look at these six verses (2:17–3:5) under the following four headings:

- There is a wrong way to struggle
- Justice is coming: two messengers
- Justice is coming: two outcomes
- There is a right way to struggle

There is a wrong way to struggle (2:17)

The people of Israel believed that they had God's blessing when they had good crops, prosperity, large and healthy families and recognition in the wider community. Their assumption was that happiness, health, prosperity and respect signified God's delight in a person. In other words, God's blessing was equated with material and earthly prosperity, whether financial, familial or communal.

Some of us in our churches hold similar views if we're not careful. We can assume that health, wealth, privilege and fame are the tokens of God's blessing. We have the idea that God's prime interest is our happiness, rather than our holiness. We believe that God's blessing is primarily for the here and now, rather than for our eternal future. We struggle with the notion that God may, in fact, choose to bless us with hardship, pain, poverty or relationship breakdown as a key route to our holiness. We are just like Malachi's contemporaries.

Malachi's contemporaries returned to the Promised Land after seventy years in exile. Whilst they were living in or around Jerusalem, with its completely rebuilt temple, much of the remainder of the city still lay in ruins. The city walls were broken down. The crops were failing, and there was widespread poverty and hunger. The nations around them gave them neither recognition nor respect; rather, they were ridiculed by those outside. They were living in despondency. As far as they were concerned, these ongoing issues were not only stark daily reminders that they had been carried into exile decades earlier, but also vivid suggestions that they were not under the blessing of God.

Furthermore, those ridiculing nations around them were seemingly happy, healthy and carefree despite practising idolatry, sexual immorality, and so on. When the people of God saw those wicked nations prospering and compared them with their own situation, they struggled. For them it looked as if God favoured the wicked and despised the righteous. As a result, they railed against God and accused him of moral upside-downness. In other words, they were struggling in the wrong way, just like the swimmer at Daytona Beach.

The devil is good at trying to persuade people that they are missing out if they are trying to live in God's way in the world. This was his tactic in the Garden of Eden back in Genesis 3, and it remains his tactic today. Christian young people go through school and university surrounded by friends who indulge in drunkenness, dabble in recreational drugs and throw themselves into intimate sexual encounters. Those same friends seem happy, wealthy, and either trouble-free or at least with no more troubles than anyone else. Thus, there is a very strong temptation for young people to feel that unless they do the same things, they will miss out. They are struggling against the rip tide of licentiousness.

Others of us wonder why we should give to the very imperfect church when doing so means that we 'miss out' on exciting holidays, extra-curricular activities for our children, new gadgets or whatever else our neighbours seem to enjoy whilst we do not.

So many of us struggle in the wrong way. And struggling this way does not get us out of the rip tide; it simply drains the life from us.

Malachi 2:17 says that the people of God were *wearying* God. Their words were exhausting him. This is astonishing: the Almighty God of heaven, who *never* sleeps, was being wearied by his people. He was tired of them. Such words pack a crippling punch. If these words do not make us stop short and think straight, it is hard to see how anything will.

In one sense, though, the fact that God was 'wearied' by them should not surprise us. Their complaints were profoundly untrue. To suggest that 'everyone who does evil is good in the sight of the LORD' (2:17) is heresy, blasphemy even. Will not the God of all the earth do right (Gen. 18:25)? And the fact that their complaints were 'wearying' to God suggests that this was no one-off event; they had been making these complaints repeatedly.

Their complaints were plain wrong because there is no straight line between God's pleasure in his people and their prosperity in this life. Equally, there is no straight line between God's displeasure in people and their suffering. The rain comes both on the just and on the unjust. Of course, there are occasions when my sin may result in my suffering (for example, if I punch you and you punch me back, my pain is a direct result of my sin). But most of the time, suffering is not the direct result of personal sin. The story of Job is a classic example of this truth.

People make the same mistake in our time, too. They look at the evils perpetrated across the world and say, 'If God really is a God of love, he wouldn't let that happen'; 'If God really cared, my husband would not have died of cancer'; or, 'If God were really there, people wouldn't get rich by squashing others.' The world is full of examples of people who reject God, strive for themselves, and tread on others in order to climb successfully the social or economic ladder. The rich elite include many who live antagonistically towards God. And, we ask, where is the justice in that?

More personally, we can think that the reason why we're having a hard time is because we don't find favour with God. When life is hard and we struggle from day to day, from hour to hour almost, we think, 'Maybe I am a really bad person whom God needs to deal with very severely.'

Malachi's contemporaries were questioning God's heart, if not his very existence: 'Where is the God of justice?' They were basically asking,

'Does he even care?' So how does God through Malachi respond to such questions?

Justice is coming: two messengers (3:1–2)

God could have responded in terms of the nations around Israel and their sinfulness. He could have outlined how he was going to bring fiery judgement upon all who reject him and live in rebellion against him. But he doesn't. Rather, he puts the spotlight on the questioners. Everything God promises to do here concerns his visible people—the ones in the church. We can point to the evils of society 'out there' and the ongoing moral decline of our country. But Malachi's message is to those *inside* the church, and that includes me (and you).

In our day, negative or unsettling news stories about churches have proliferated. Not long ago, the Methodist Church issued a full apology as it completed a full inquiry into sexual abuse within that Church over the previous fifty-year period. As we are painfully aware, the Methodist Church is not alone in exposing this kind of sin found within its ranks. Another clear example of moral decline in the church in the UK is its endorsement of, or at least silence on, the world's normalization of sexual practice outside marriage. The church worries about standing for truth or moral integrity, concerned it will permanently earn such labels as bigoted, intolerant, even dangerous, in addition to its current label, 'irrelevant'.

Malachi 2:17 began with a megaphoned question about God's justice: is God really just? But the rest of the disputation burns hot in response: yes, God is just. 'But who can endure the day of his coming, and who can stand when he appears?' (3:2). Will *you* be able to stand when he comes to bring justice? God's primary concern here is not the purging of the nations, but the purifying of his people.

Look how God through Malachi responds to the people's questioning in 3:1. He talks about two messengers of God.

- First, he describes God's messenger who will 'prepare the way' before him.
- Second, he describes the messenger of the covenant who will 'come to his temple'.

Who are these messengers?

The first messenger

Jesus himself discusses the first messenger. In Matthew 11:10, when talking about John the Baptist, Jesus says, 'This is he of whom it is written: "Behold, I send my messenger before your face, who will prepare your way before you."' Jesus is quoting this verse from Malachi and applying it to John the Baptist. John the Baptist was this first messenger. What was the role of this first messenger? To prepare the way.

Mark (see Mark 1:2) puts this Malachi verse alongside the words of Isaiah:

> A voice cries:
> 'In the wilderness prepare the way of the LORD;
>> make straight in the desert a highway for our God.
> Every valley shall be lifted up,
>> and every mountain and hill be made low;
> the uneven ground shall become level,
>> and the rough places a plain.
> And the glory of the LORD shall be revealed,
>> and all flesh shall see it together,
>> for the mouth of the LORD has spoken.' (Isa. 40:3–5)

Mark put these verses together because he knew that when any Jew heard about one who would prepare the way of the Lord, they would instantly think of Isaiah's prophecy about the coming Messiah.

In Isaiah, the context was the wilderness—the place where the way of the Lord would be prepared. Here in Malachi, the context is also one of drought, but also poverty due to bad crops and lack of rain. So this

Isaianic messenger seems very pertinent to their condition. Four hundred years after Malachi, John the Baptist arrived on the scene. Not only did he come as the last in the line of prophets, he also embodied his own prophetic message. The people of God were in a state of subjugation under Rome, down-trodden and spiritually in the wilderness. And John the Baptist burst onto the scene by way of the wilderness, wearing camels' hair and eating simple food, the clothing and food of repentance. Thus he shouted with his very being that these people who were in the spiritual wilderness needed to repent, and he proclaimed it loud and clear in words as well: 'Repent, for the kingdom of heaven is at hand' (Matt. 3:2). John's role was to call people to repentance.

But what about the second messenger?

The second messenger

In Malachi 3:1 we also read of a second messenger, 'the messenger of the covenant', described in this verse as 'the Lord whom you seek', who will 'come to *his* temple'. This second messenger is the Messiah, God himself. The first messenger prepares the way for the Lord; the second messenger *is* the Lord.

Notice the contrast between 3:1 and 2:17. In 2:17 the people argue that God delights in those who do evil, because he allows them to prosper (the NIV uses the words 'pleased with', but it is really 'delights in'—a much stronger accusation). But then in 3:1 God turns it around: 'the messenger of the covenant in whom *you* delight [same word in the original], behold, he is coming.'

You want justice? Justice is coming, says God. There is something ominous about the way God says that. The use of the word 'suddenly' earlier in the verse alerts us to the fact that something to do with judgement is about to be discussed. Then it comes in verse 2: he is coming, but who can endure the day of his coming? Who can stand when he appears?

Verse 2 is starkly different from verse 1 because it changes suddenly from the prose of verse 1 into full-blown Hebrew poetry. In the original, the effect is jarring. All of a sudden, the questions of Malachi's contemporaries regarding the justice of God are turned around and focused upon them: 'Justice is coming. And who will be able to stand. You?'

So justice is coming by way of two messengers—John the Baptist and Jesus himself. But what do we know about this coming judgement?

Justice is coming: two outcomes (3:3–5)

The messenger of the covenant, the 'judge', is going to refine and purify, and he is going to start with the sons of Levi (3:3). The priests were engaged in syncretism—they were 'woolly round the edges', lackadaisical, lacking in zeal for the Lord. They were offering unsacrificial sacrifices and failing to demand holiness from God's people. God has already spoken against them in 1:6–2:9. But now, God says he is going to send his messenger whose job it is to purify them.

Think about what Jesus did during his first coming. He spent a good deal of time railing against the religious insiders who didn't recognize their own sinfulness and need of salvation. He called them 'whitewashed tombs', looking good on the outside, but with rotting flesh within. Remember that Jesus cleared the temple both at the beginning and at the end of his ministry. He came 'suddenly' to his temple. Jesus did a good deal of refining when he first came, and it was particularly directed at the priests, the sons of Levi, who failed to recognize him and failed to enact justice and lead in a godly way. He came against the Pharisees, the Sadducees and the teachers of the law again and again.

It is tempting to think that this ministry was fruitless (apart, perhaps, from Nicodemus). However, following his resurrection, after the explosion in the growth of the church in Acts 2, Luke tells us that 'the word of God continued to increase, and the number of the disciples multiplied greatly in Jerusalem, and *a great many of the priests became obedient to the faith*' (Acts 6:7). Perhaps Jesus' ministry was not fruitless after all—it just took a while for the seed to sprout. A large number of priests, the ones he railed against during his ministry, became obedient to Jesus.

Why does Malachi focus on the purifying of the priests, the sons of Levi? Because as the leaders go, so go the people. Since people follow their leaders, God is committed to sanctifying the leaders first of all. If we desire to live holy lives dedicated to the Lord and be effective in ministry, we must pray for the holiness and purifying of our leaders. We must pray for our leaders—for those who preach, teach or lead—that God would work in them, so that they might be increasingly able to serve well and reflect Jesus aright.

These words probably refer not just to Jesus' first coming but also to his second coming. It might have been an easier message if Malachi had finished after verse 4 and moved right onto the fifth disputation in verse 6. But he didn't. In verse 5, Malachi continues to fix his gaze on God's people: 'I will draw near to *you* for judgement.' The issues are still *within the visible people of God*. This is a strong warning to the church: God's primary desire is to purge the evil from within the gathered people. Would the people of Malachi's day be refined in the fire and purified—disciplined unto life—as reflected in 3:2–4? Or would they be judged and condemned—judgement unto death—as reflected in 3:5? And what about us? Will we be refined and purified fully, or will we face his condemnation? If you go to a local church, make sure you really are part of the universal church. Malachi's point is that if you are not truly part of God's family, you will face, not discipline unto life, but judgement unto death. This death-judgement is for those who continue to fail to fear the Lord.

So there are two outcomes to the judgement: discipline unto life, or judgement unto death. Notice that God's judgement falls on all sorts of people in 3:6. Those who practise sorcery are aligning themselves with

Chapter 4

Satan. Those who practise adultery are tearing apart God's covenantal
bonds. Those who perjure themselves, who oppress the workers, who
ignore widows and orphans, who thrust aside the sojourner—all these
stand utterly against God. Each of these fails to fear God, to trust in God,
to obey God. And God is a swift witness against them in judgement.

At the end of Malachi 3:3, in the phrase 'they will bring offerings in
righteousness to the LORD', the original language has a deliberate double
meaning. First, Malachi is describing the quality of the offerings
themselves: they will be right sacrifices once more. But he is also
describing the way in which those offerings are brought: those making
the offerings will be righteous. Why will they be righteous? Because the
Lord has refined, purified, them. That's the only route to righteousness:
it is the work of God. You cannot purify yourself. The silver doesn't jump
into the furnace and heat itself up; God must do the work. Our role is to
submit to his refining work. And then he makes us right, both immediately
(by giving us the righteousness of Jesus) and continually (as he works in
us to make us more holy).

What an encouragement this is! We welcome the truth that justification
is by faith alone and not by works (see Eph. 2:8–10). In our day, though,
many of us believe that once we are converted, it does not matter
particularly what we do—our eternal destiny is secure. But Paul writes,
'Are we to continue in sin that grace may abound? By no means!' (Rom.
6:1–2). In theological terms, justification is not a means to avoid
sanctification—it is the only road *into* sanctification. Once we come to
trust in Jesus, we should become more and more like Jesus. Paul writes
lucidly: 'Work out your own salvation with fear and trembling...' (Phil.
2:12b). Once I become a Christian, my role is to work out my salvation—
to work *hard* at growing to be more like Jesus. Paul writes elsewhere, 'I
discipline my body and keep it under control, lest after preaching to
others I myself should be disqualified' (1 Cor. 9:27).

At the same time, we note that 'Work out your own salvation with fear and trembling' (Phil. 2:12b) is not the whole of Paul's sentence. Yes, as Christians we need to work hard at our sanctification and to grow more like Jesus, but ultimately this is not something *we* do: '. . . for it is God who works in you, both to will and to work for his good pleasure' (Phil. 2:13). It is *God* who works in us. It is he who works in us the desire ('to will') to follow him as well as the actual works ('to work') which follow from the desire. If we don't desire to serve Jesus, we'll never be able to serve him from the heart and so our 'good works' will never bring him pleasure. But God changes our desires! That should be the heart of our prayer against temptation to sin: 'Lord, change my desires. Lord, grow my heart to love you alone. Lord, change my deepest longing so that it would be for you alone.' As God changes our desires, so our works will change—not because *we* do it, but because God does it in us. Ultimately, the Christian life is about God working in us to *will* and to work for his good pleasure. He refines us, purifies us and makes us righteous as we strive to live for him.

This messenger of the covenant to whom Malachi refers—Jesus—will both purify and purge! People who are not really his will be purged and punished; those who *are* his, he will purify. Malachi tells us the result of this purifying process in 3:3b–4: 'They will bring offerings in righteousness to the LORD. Then the offering of Judah and Jerusalem will be pleasing to the LORD as in the days of old and as in former years.' As God refines us, so our offerings will be pleasing to him.

God is going to restore his people to spiritual life. If you are part of the church but not really *of* the church, not belonging to God, Malachi is blunt: in the end, the weeds will be separated from the wheat and be burned up in the fire as God purifies his people. The point of Malachi's words is simple: don't be a weed! We need to turn from our rebelliousness to Jesus so that he will save us. I must ask for his life-giving work to begin in me, because only then will I not be burned up.

So we've seen how God responded to Malachi's contemporaries

struggling in the wrong way. But how does that help us to struggle in the right way?

There is a right way to struggle

It is useful to refer to Psalm 73 here because there is a stark contrast between the people of Malachi's day and the words of Asaph in Psalm 73.

Asaph writes with conviction in the first verse, 'Truly God is good to Israel, to those who are pure in heart.' But then he goes on to recognize his struggles with what he sees around him:

> But as for me, my feet had almost stumbled;
>
> my steps had nearly slipped.
>
> For I was envious of the arrogant
>
> when I saw the prosperity of the wicked. (vv. 2–3)

Too often I find myself doing the very same thing. I think that if I indulged in the sin of those around me, somehow that would be good for me! Perhaps I even *envy* the sin of the wicked. Those who do not live God's way seem to enjoy life so much.

However, there is a huge difference between what is happening in Psalm 73 and the complaints we find back in Malachi 2:17. Malachi's contemporaries shout direct accusations at God; Asaph wonders about them in his heart. Malachi's contemporaries look only at the sins of others; Asaph knows his own sin, too. Malachi's contemporaries look only to the present; Asaph has a broader historical perspective, from the past to the future. Malachi's contemporaries do not trust God at all; Asaph not only trusts in God, he delights in God.

Asaph does not shout out in arrogance, 'God is not just'; he reminds himself of the eternal perspective. He remembers the destiny of all those who reject God: that they will be cast down into ruin. They will have their comeuppance (Ps. 73:17–19). And he reminds himself of his own destiny, in which God will take him to glory (v. 24). He recognizes that his questions are senseless and ignorant (v. 22) and so he relaxes peacefully into the arms of his loving Lord:

> Whom have I in heaven but you?
>
> And there is nothing on earth that I desire besides you.
>
> My flesh and my heart may fail [I am sinful and fail often; I am faint-hearted and weak in faith],
>
> but God is the strength of my heart and my portion for ever. (vv. 25–26)

Whilst the questions and struggles of Asaph and of Malachi's contemporaries are the same, their hearts are different. Asaph keeps quiet, struggles on, and somehow trusts in God. But the words of Malachi's contemporaries belie their heart condition. Underneath their complaint is a misguided belief that they are following God and deserve his favour. But this is patently untrue. We have already considered their corrupt leaders, their unsacrificial sacrifices, their unfaithful personal relationships and their rejection of God's design for marriage.

Behind the accusation against God—'You are not just'—lies their failure to recognize their own sinfulness and to acknowledge God's holiness and justice as true, however it may seem from their perspective.

So how do we avoid the error of Malachi's contemporaries? Should we pretend we don't have questions? No. Should we try really hard to have enough faith? No. Should we ignore the pain and struggles of life? No. Should we ignore the fact that evil people prosper and good people suffer? No. Should we somehow numb ourselves to suffering and claim it doesn't affect us? No. Rather, we should acknowledge our questions, the reality of the pain, the flagrant sin of others and the lies of Satan that the things of this world will make us wise.

But also we must broaden our perspective. We must remind ourselves: 'How has God blessed me in the past? What has the Lord done for me in the past?' This will take us back to many wonderful things we have experienced during our Christian walk. It will remind us of when we were first saved—when we first submitted to Jesus and asked for his forgiveness. But it will take us ever further back: to the way he worked in us to bring us to the point of salvation; to God's protection and sustaining of us throughout life; to God's design in bringing us into the world; to the Lord Jesus himself and his cross, where he took upon himself the wrath of God and exchanged his righteousness for our wickedness, and our punishment for his own harrowing death; and even to the very dawn of time, when God created all things and said, even then, 'You will be mine.' Looking back is helpful in broadening our perspective.

But we will also look forward: to the day when, in the words of Asaph, 'Those who are far from [God] shall perish; [God puts] an end to everyone who is unfaithful to [him]' (Ps. 73:27); to that day when judgement will finally come; and to that day when, afterwards, God will bring us into glory. Whom have we in heaven but Jesus? Earth has nothing, *nothing*, I desire besides him. My flesh and my heart may fail—I may fall into sin, I may die—but God is the strength of my heart.

Like Asaph, we avoid the sin of Malachi's contemporaries by delighting in God.

Conclusion

Consider once again Malachi's contemporaries. They accused God and struggled in the wrong way. God responded by telling them that justice would be done. When I first looked at this, I wondered, 'How did God's response to their bold questions of 2:17 help *them* in their situation?' This messenger Malachi was talking about wouldn't arrive for another four hundred years. None of those people asking the question would see the fulfilment of this prophecy—they'd all be long gone. So how was it helpful for God to tell them this messenger was coming? Similarly for us, 2,400 years later: how does knowing that God is going to bring final judgement eventually (however many years from now) help us in our struggles in our day? Malachi 2:17–3:5 highlights two clear responses to this question.

Patience

The first way it helps us is by showing us the patience of God. He could bring his judgement right now, but he does not. Why not? Because he is patient. Peter makes the same point: 'The Lord is not slow to fulfil his promise as some count slowness, but is patient towards you, not wishing that any should perish, but that all should reach repentance' (2 Peter 3:9; see the whole of 3:3–9). Peter saw scoffers in his day, too. He says, 'Don't forget to broaden your perspective: look backwards and forwards. Judgement will come. But God is patient with you, not wanting anyone to perish, but everyone to come to repentance.'

God promises that justice will be done. But he withholds it at the moment, for our good. If God were to bring his justice upon the world now, and you are not living in submission to Jesus, all hope would be gone for you. In the famous image of Jonathan Edwards, you dangle over the fire of hell, and the only reason you do not fall is that God continues to hold you and wait for you to come in repentance to him.[1] God is patient. In the case of our friends and loved ones who are not yet converted, we may praise God that Jesus is not coming right now. Praise God for his patience and his faithfulness: it means there is still hope. God's patience is a huge blessing. He was patient towards us, and we are grateful he continues in patience towards others.

If you are dangling, as Edwards put it, do not presume upon God's patience. There is no time to be lost: today is the day of salvation. Trust in him, and thank him for his patience.

For those of us who are Christians, we are glad of God's patience towards us, too—he is slowly changing us to be the people he wants us to be. Slowly he is dealing with our sin. Slowly he is moulding our characters. I am thankful for his patience in dealing with me, a tough sin-criminal who needs strong, hard and lengthy work.

Knowing that final judgement is coming helps us in another way, too.

Surprise!

Enshrined in the words of Malachi we find God's warning that judgement will come suddenly: 'The LORD whom you seek will *suddenly* come to his temple' (3:1); 'I will be *quick* to testify . . . ' (3:5, NIV). The word 'suddenly' does not mean soon or imminently; it means unexpectedly or surprisingly. When Jesus came the first time it was not soon or imminent, but it was unexpected and surprising. And when he comes for the second time, it will be equally surprising and unexpected, like a thief in the night—not to take things from us, but to take us to himself.

Peter picks up on this, too: '[The Lord] is patient towards you, not wishing that any should perish, but that all should reach repentance. But the day of the Lord will come like a thief' (2 Peter 3:9–10). This is a warning to the not-yet-Christian. Some time—nobody knows when— Jesus will come back. Are you ready? And it is a help to the Christian. We do not know when Jesus will return. All we know is that it will be sudden, perhaps soon. Certainly it will be sooner for us than it was for those in Malachi's day or Peter's day. Are we ready?

There's a wrong way to struggle in the sea: a struggling that means the current takes you out, you struggle fruitlessly and it leads to death. There is a wrong way to struggle as a Christian, too: a struggle that accepts salvation by faith alone but disregards sanctification by faith alone. But there is a way to struggle that is right: a sacred struggle. This struggle is one in which we pray for God to grow our desire, love and yearning for him alone. This struggle keeps a broad perspective, trusting in him day by day, delighting in the God of justice who will, one day, make all things new and bring everything to its just and right conclusion. As we struggle, we must keep our perspective.

Finally, this is not some theoretical idea in the mind of God. Think of Jesus' truly sacred struggle, as God-made-man in this fallen and sin-stained world. Think of his struggle in the Garden of Gethsemane. How did Jesus make it through his arrest, torture and murder? How did he endure it? He prayed. He sweated blood in prayer. In essence, his prayer was to embody the will of his Father as his deepest joy. He kept a broad perspective and kept his focus on and delight in God. Let's encourage one another to live that way, too. Pray hard; and keep a broad perspective, delighting in God.

It is only because of him who loves us and sought to bring us salvation that we can be confident that 'it is well with my soul'.[2] Our circumstances may attack us from all angles; the people we love may spit in our faces. But the messenger of the covenant has borne our sin and is purifying us, so, in the end, it is well with our souls.

Notes

1 Jonathan Edwards, 'Sinners in the Hands of an Angry God', 1741, http://www.jonathan-edwards.org/Sinners.pdf.

2 Horatio Spafford, 'When Peace Like a River', 1873.

Money matters: the giving of God (3:6–12)

There is a story of a pastor who appeared at a morning service fully dressed in police riot gear, complete with a riot shield. His parishioners watched in fascination as the last notes of the hymn faded away and their pastor mounted the platform. He moved to the pulpit and asked the people to turn to Malachi 3:6–12. He was about to preach on the subject of giving, so he had come prepared!

Malachi 3:6–12 does indeed have much to say about the subject of giving, and God's words through Malachi challenge us to reconsider our approach to financial giving. Indeed, Malachi's writing in this chapter pushes particularly hard against our materialistic Western world, so we will need to spend considerable time on this thorny subject. However, money is not the only concern in these seven verses. There are deeper things at stake, too—things concerning the nature of repentance, the essence of worship and the character of God himself.

God does not change (3:6–7)

This section begins with a key statement about God: 'I the LORD do not change.' This is a hugely important doctrine, which is sometimes called the immutability of God. God doesn't change. This means he is unchanging in his mind, in his will and in his nature.

It has been argued that change involves time—a point before the change and a point after the change—so to suggest that God changed would suggest he was in some way bound by time. More compellingly, for God to change morally suggests an imperfection in God. For example, a change from one thing to a better thing would mean that before the change, God was less than perfect. Likewise, a change from one thing to something not so good would also mean an imperfection in God now. The argument is that if God is perfect in every way, it is vital that he retains that perfection and so does not change, otherwise he would be a fallen and fallible God.

God is also unchanging in his character. The fruit of the Spirit in all its facets (love, joy, peace, patience, kindness, goodness, faithfulness, gentleness, self-control) is the character of God as well as the character God seeks to work in us if we are his children. God is always all of these things. He is also *always* perfectly holy, just, right, true, admirable, excellent and praiseworthy. The immutability of God is a wonderful truth.

But how is God's immutability connected with the situation and experiences of his people? Why does God make this doctrinal point here in Malachi 3:6? The structure of the verse helps us find the answer. The verse is put together as a classic Hebrew couplet and basically reads, 'Since I the Lord do not change, so you, descendants of Jacob, are not destroyed.' In other words, (a) God's unchanging will means he *does not wish to* destroy them; (b) his unchanging character (his patience) means *he will not* destroy them; and (c) his covenant promises stand firm and so *he cannot* destroy them. The immutability of God is a huge comfort to his people amidst their sinfulness.

It is a similar comfort to us today, too. If we have turned away from our sinful past and towards the Lord Jesus alone for our salvation, then the character of God himself means that he does not wish to destroy us, he will not destroy us and he cannot destroy us. These things hold true regardless of our sinfulness. So if I find myself falling into temptation yet again, or messing up my relationships with others, nevertheless I will never be destroyed. I am 'safe' and will spend eternity with the Lord Jesus, not because of my own righteousness, but because of the immutability of God. It is because *God* does not change that we will be saved. Such a wonderful truth drives us deeper in our love for Jesus, and the result is that we grow more and more like him. Anyone who says 'I can behave however I like now because I know I am saved' has failed to understand what repentance and faith are all about.

Notice that God labels his people the 'children of Jacob' in 3:6. This is the same description we noted back in chapter 1. They are children of the deceiver, the usurper, the schemer, the one who lied and cheated and stole his brother's birthright. Sadly, the children of Jacob are like their father. The word for 'fathers' in 3:7 can mean fathers, grandfathers or great-grandfathers, so the point God is making in 3:6–7 is twofold and clear. First, God has not changed, and that is a good thing because God is perfect. Second, the people have not changed either, and that is a very bad thing, because they are deeply sinful.

The people continue to be 'children of Jacob' the deceiver. God does not and must not change; but they *must* change. They have not followed God (i.e. they deserve God's punishment), but God's covenant promises remain firm and they are not destroyed even though they are still rebellious. So how can the 'children of Jacob' become the children of God? How can they change? It is this question that Malachi answers next.

Salvation comes through repentance (3:7–10)

What does it mean to 'return'?

In 3:7 we read that the people have turned away from God ('you have turned aside from my statutes') *and* God has turned away from them. When he says, 'Return to me, and I will return to you,' we need to note that the word 'return' in the original Hebrew means to 'turn back'. God can only turn *back* to them if he has turned *away* from them in the past. We have seen evidence of God's 'turning away' already in Malachi 1:10b: 'I have no pleasure in you, says the LORD of hosts, and I will not accept an offering from your hand.' In 2:13, God 'no longer regards the offering or accepts it with favour from [their] hand'. Why not? Because of their sin.

God has turned away from them because they have turned away from him: 'you have turned aside from the way' (2:8); 'abomination has been committed in Israel' (2:11); 'you . . . despise my name' (1:6); 'You have wearied the LORD' (2:17). In essence, they are apart from him at the moment. But God calls them to return to him in the knowledge that if they do so, he will return to them.

Whilst it is true that they have systematically and repeatedly turned away from God, God's turning away from them is not an ultimate rejection. Rather, it is a fulfilment of the covenant curses which were to come upon his people if they turned away from the covenant. Think back to Leviticus 26. In that chapter, God was clear that if his people rebelled, he would punish them. If they continued to rebel, he would punish them more. If they *still* continued to rebel, he would punish them even more. But the aim at each stage was to bring about repentance—turning back to God. If they turned back, then God would bless them.

We see this fulfilled most completely at the cross. Jesus, the only person ever to have lived a perfect life, hung on the cross and took upon himself all of our sin, rebellion, hatred, anger, lust, violence, greed and laziness. God the Father turned his face away from him, so Jesus cried out, 'My God, my God, why have you abandoned me?' The fulfilment of the covenantal curse which we deserve is for God's face to be turned away. For each of us, one of two things will happen at the end of time: either God's face will be turned away from us and we'll face eternal destruction, or his face will already have been turned away from Jesus as Jesus bore our sin and took the punishment we deserve. The aim of God's temporal punishments in Leviticus and in Malachi was to persuade his people to repent—to turn back to him. God had turned away for the moment: this is the covenantal 'curse' God speaks of in Malachi 3:9. If we live in sin, God stands apart from us.

God turns away from his people in order that they will repent, so when God calls them to return to him he promises that if they do, he will *re*turn to them. This is a precursor to the story of the Prodigal Son in Luke 15. The son rejected his father, took all the riches his father had to offer and ran away to spend his inheritance in wild living. He was separated from his father, as he wanted to be. He thought that rejecting his father and going his own way would make him happy. But he was wrong. And one day, when he was virtually destitute, feeding the pigs, he came to his senses. He realized that turning *away* from his father meant turning *towards* destruction. And so he turned and headed back to his father. The wonderful part of the story is the response of his father. Whilst the son was still a long way off, his father *ran* towards him to welcome him home.

In the ancient Near East, fathers would never run. They were the head of the family and esteemed in society. If they were late, people would be expected to wait for them. Further, because they wore long robes, in order to run they would need to hitch up their skirts, exposing their underwear (underwear was long, too!)—a shameful thing for a father to do. But in the story of the Prodigal Son, when the son who had rejected his father, squandered his father's wealth, betrayed his trust and effectively told him 'I wish you were dead' now appears on the horizon, astoundingly, the father takes shame upon himself and runs to embrace his son.

Perhaps this is your experience, too? Perhaps you have run from God, spent your life turned against him in wild living—either overtly so everyone could see it, or covertly in your head and heart, slowly but relentlessly driving against God. But you came to your senses, too. You turned back towards home. And the heavenly Father came running to embrace you. In fact, this is the experience of every Christian. We were rebellious and against our heavenly Father. But now we have been brought near and embraced by him. As we walked towards him, he came running over the brow of the hill with his arms wide open.

So how does this 'return' happen?

How can a person 'return'?

The next part of Malachi is fascinating. We might expect the answer to the question 'How do I come back to God?' to be, 'Repent.' How do you return to the Lord? You ask for his forgiveness and you commit yourself to Jesus. But Malachi doesn't seem to say this at all.

In fact, he actually says that the people are under God's curse because they are not giving the tithe. The Law of Moses stated that one tenth part of all they had was to be given back to God, usually via the temple. God's people were failing to give in this way, and, according to Malachi 3:8–9, it was for this reason that they lay under God's curse. This sounds like serious USA tele-evangelism, doesn't it? Give your money to us and God will return to you. If you give more, God will listen to you.

It seems to get worse, too: 'Bring the full tithe into the storehouse, that there may be food in my house. And thereby put me to the test, says the LORD of hosts, if I will not open the windows of heaven for you and pour down for you a blessing until there is no more need' (v. 10). Is Malachi saying, 'Give to God, and he'll give back to you'? Is he saying, 'Blessing comes to you if you give to us'? If so, this feels like a full-blown prosperity gospel: God wants you to be happy; he wants to bless you. And if you would only give sacrificially, he will bless you a hundredfold.

One American televangelist caused a stir a while back when a crowdfunding campaign asked 200,000 of its international supporters to donate $300 each so that they could purchase a $60m private jet, ostensibly to further their global ministry. 'Give and you will receive. Give to God and he will bless you a hundredfold.' Is that really the point God is making through Malachi?

No—not even vaguely. So what is Malachi's point, here? Why does tithing seem to be such a central issue? The gospel is not, 'Repent and be baptized, every one of you, and give your tithe, for the forgiveness of your sins.' Neither is it, 'Whoever believes in him and gives their tithe shall not perish but have eternal life.' So why is Malachi fixated on the tithe?

The fact is that in the Old Testament, two words are used for repentance, and one of them is used right here.[1] We have noted it already: it is the word 'return', and it is all about repentance. It means to 'turn back'. Repentance means turning back from sin towards God.

We sometimes forget the binary nature of repentance. If we turn towards God, we turn away from sin. If we turn away from God, we are walking into sin. They are simultaneous events. So to 'turn back' to God is to 'turn away' from sin—and that, of course, is the essence of repentance.

So in Malachi 3:7, 'return to me [God]' really means, 'repent to God'. The 'returning' phrase is explicitly about repentance. I think that one reason why the translators opted to translate the word as 'return' is because the same word is used of God: 'return to me, and I will return to you'. We would baulk at a translation 'repent to me, and I will repent to you'! But to 'turn back' to God is a good thing, suggesting that the people had turned away from God, which is the essence of sin. And for God to 'turn back' to them is a good thing, too. God had turned away, not because of his sin, but because of *their* sin. They had sinned, so he turned away. For God to 'repent' implies not that God has his own sin to turn from, but that he may now turn towards someone because their sin is no longer in the way. For a person to repent to God means they recognize their own fallenness and brokenness and turn away from their sin. If our sin is dealt with, God can turn back to us.

Another reason why the translators used 'return' instead of 'repent' lies in the question the people ask: 'How shall we return?', and in God's answer: 'In your tithes and contributions.' Good translators know that repentance is not primarily to do with giving money. So they chose 'return' instead of 'repent'.

The question the people are asking, though, is really, 'What do we need to repent of? All those heathen out there—they've got loads to repent of. But we're not like them. Why do we need to repent?' So God gives them a specific, concrete, ongoing and repeated sin in which they're engaged: selfishness with their money. They *do* actually need to repent.

When John the Baptist came calling for repentance for the forgiveness of sins, he didn't mention money (Matt. 3:2). And again, in Acts 2, when Peter calls, 'Repent and be baptized every one of you . . . for the forgiveness of your sins' (Acts 2:38), money is not mentioned.

But sometimes money is mentioned, because it has everything to do with repentance. Consider the rich man who wanted to follow Jesus. 'I have kept all the commandments since I was a boy,' he says (see Mark 10:20). What does Jesus say? 'Go, sell all that you have and give it to the poor . . . and come, follow me' (10:21). For the rich man, repentance was intimately tied up with money. Why? Because the deepest and most precious idol to him was money; and if we are to turn towards God in repentance, all idols must be left at the door. If I turn towards God, I turn away from sin. You cannot serve both God and something else, including money. A once-respected pastor said, 'Jesus plus nothing equals everything', and he was right. Jesus plus something else is idolatry. How hard it is for a rich man to enter the kingdom of heaven! Why? Because the idol of wealth drives deep anchors into the soul.

So repentance is about turning towards God and away from whatever binds us, whatever we hold as an idol. For the priests in Jesus' day, it was religious prestige and image that held them, so his call to repentance involved castigating them about hypocrisy: they needed to be right on the inside and not be whitewashed tombs. In Malachi's day, the people and the priests were bringing unsacrificial sacrifices. They didn't want to part with their money (the little they had of it)—they wanted to do worship on the cheap. So, in order for them to repent, the idol of wealth had to be broken. Hence Malachi probes into tithing; for them, repentance and money were deeply connected.

There's a further reason why Malachi tackles tithing and giving. Let's remind ourselves what the tithe actually was.

Stuart points out that for the Old Testament worship system to work, 10 per cent giving on the part of the people was necessary.[2] The Levites formed around a twelfth of the population, so they would need around 8.3 per cent of the national income in order to be supported. The cost of the upkeep of the temple and its furnishings came from the tithe. Further, tithes were meant to help provide for the poor, the orphans, the widows, and so on. Importantly, all the people were meant to tithe, including the priests and Levites. Perhaps that is an important message for those who are paid to work for the church: tithing isn't required only of those in the pew; it is required of every Christian.

A full 10 per cent from everyone was needed to keep the system running; 9 per cent would not be enough. Why was tithing important? Because without it, those set apart to lead the people in their spiritual lives would be unable to do so. Without the tithe, the widow, the orphan and the poor would have no means of support, and the priests and Levites would be unable to survive. And, without the tithe, there were insufficient funds for maintenance of the temple and supply of oil, incense, altar fuel, and so on. So both ministry and mission would be impossible without the tithe. At root, the tithe was required in order for collective worship to be possible.

Worship is the basic, initial and permanent response of the believer to God, and to fail to tithe was to hinder and undermine their ability to worship as they should.

Exodus 19:5 reminds us that all the earth, and everything in it, is the Lord's. Psalm 50:10 tells us that God owns the cattle on a thousand hills. In a sense, all of creation belongs to God because God created it. But God gave people the task of stewarding his creation, of ruling over it. Leviticus 27:30 tells us that the tithe belongs to God. Whatever resulted from people farming the land—crops or animals which the Lord had blessed and made fruitful—10 per cent of that belonged immediately and inherently to God.

A sacrifice of worship (3:8–10)

Malachi is arguing here that failing to give the tithe equates to stealing from God (3:8). If we are to worship rightly, giving is an essential part of that. If I am not giving right, I am not worshipping right.

God knows the penchant of the human heart towards greed. It has rightly been said, 'Check a person's bank statement and you check the state of their heart.' Jesus echoes this with, 'Where your treasure is, there your heart will be also' (Matt. 6:21).

In Malachi 3:8–9, God promises that if they tithe fully, and contribute on top of that ('tithes *and* contributions'), he will bring them ongoing blessing. The Hebrew of verse 10 really reads, 'See if I will not open the windows of heaven for you and pour down for you a blessing until failure of sufficiency'—that is, 'until the sufficiency of God runs out'. The idea is one of blessings to satisfy our needs in perpetuity. This is not God endorsing the prosperity gospel; he is not saying, 'Give me money and I will make you rich!' Rather, God is promising that if they keep on giving, he will keep on blessing.

Some history helps us here. Think back to the time of King Hezekiah. Hezekiah became king about 140 years before the fall of Jerusalem and consequent exile in Babylon. When he became king, he brought about a series of reforms to return the people to worshipping God aright. Many kings before him had led the people away from God, but Hezekiah wanted to put this right. So he got the temple doors repaired, had everything removed that should not be there, and cleansed and purified the temple. He got the priests to consecrate themselves.

Once everything was done, he got the people together and went with them up to the temple. They made the sacrifices required by the law—in fact, they made abundantly more than that. The band had been rehearsing and played music as soon as the sacrifices began. Then we read in 2 Chronicles 29:27, 'Hezekiah commanded that the burnt offering be offered on the altar.' As the offering began, singing to the Lord also began, accompanied by trumpets and the instruments of David, king of Israel. The whole assembly bowed in worship while the singers sang and the trumpeters played. All this continued until the sacrifice of the burnt offering was completed. When the offerings were finished, the king and everyone present with him knelt down and worshipped. King Hezekiah and his officials ordered the Levites to praise the LORD with the words of David and of Asaph the seer. They therefore 'sang praises with gladness, and they bowed down and worshipped . . . Thus the service of the house of the LORD was restored' (29:30, 35). Next, Hezekiah reinstituted the Passover festival, and then destroyed all the idols and altars to Baal and the Asherah poles. Then everyone returned home.

But look what happened next: 'Hezekiah appointed the divisions of the priests and of the Levites . . . for burnt offerings and peace offerings, to minister in the gates of the camp of the Lord' (2 Chr. 31:2). Then the king contributed from his own possessions for the morning and evening burnt offerings. He ordered the people living in Jerusalem 'to give the portion due to the priests and the Levites, that they might give themselves to the Law of the LORD [i.e. to the Scriptures]' (31:4). As soon as the order went out, the Israelites generously gave 'the firstfruits of grain, wine, oil, honey, and of all the produce of the field. And they brought in abundantly the tithe of everything' (v. 5). The men of Israel and Judah brought their tithe and piled it in heaps (v. 6). Then, when Hezekiah and his officials came and saw the heaps, they praised the Lord and blessed God's people Israel (v. 8).

The chief priest said to Hezekiah: 'Since they began to bring the contributions into the house of the Lord, we have eaten and had enough and have plenty left.' Why? '*For the* LORD *has blessed his people*' (31:10). So they built storerooms to save the contributions and distribute them as needed. 'Thus Hezekiah did throughout all Judah, and he did what was good and right and faithful before the LORD his God. And every work that he undertook in the service of the house of God and in accordance with the law and the commandments, seeking his God, he did with all his heart, and prospered' (vv. 20–21).

My wife and I's experience through our married life has been that when we honour God with our finances, God honours us by providing for our needs. Malachi is very clear here that to not give the full tithe is to rob God. Many people say, 'Tithing is Old Testament—we don't have to do it any more,' but this is not a logical argument. Tithing does come from the Old Testament, but so, too, do commands such as 'Do not murder'! We must not assume that if something appears in the Old Testament law, it no longer applies. There are at least two further reasons why this logic is flawed when applied to the principle of tithing.

First, tithing was in place long before the Law of Moses was given at Sinai. Think back to Genesis 14. Abraham had gone into battle to rescue his nephew Lot. Following this battle, Melchizedek came down to him from Salem (a name which means 'peace') with bread and wine as refreshment. Melchizedek's name means 'king of righteousness', and his role was as priest of God Most High at Salem (Salem would later become Jerusalem). So Melchizedek, king of righteousness, king of peace and priest of God Most High, brought bread and wine to Abraham. Thus, Melchizedek was a picture of what Jesus would be and do when he came two thousand years later. Jesus, the great King of Righteousness, the true Prince of Peace and our great High Priest of God, sat in the upper room offering bread and wine as a foreshadowed memorial of his self-sacrifice on our behalf. The story of Melchizedek is a beautiful and rich treasure, filled with the aroma of Christ.

After receiving the bread and wine, Abraham gave Melchizedek, the priest of God, a tithe of all he had, 10 per cent of everything. This was the logical thing to do. Remember that Abraham preceded Moses by many centuries. So tithing did not begin with the Law of Moses; it began a long time before that.

There is a further, second reason why I think tithing remains a biblical mandate. There *is* a New Testament text that says a little bit about tithing. Jesus said, 'Woe to you, scribes and Pharisees, hypocrites! For you tithe mint and dill and cumin, and have neglected the weightier matters of the law: justice and mercy and faithfulness. These you ought to have done, without neglecting the former' (Matt. 23:23; Luke 11:42). Jesus is not saying that people shouldn't tithe; in fact, he's specifically stating the opposite: 'You should have practised the latter, *without neglecting the former.*' You're still expected to tithe, but without forgetting the even more important matters of justice, mercy and faithfulness.

Tithing at the very least is expected of us. In the Old Testament, people were meant to look at the kindness and generosity of God and give back to him a tenth of all they had. Now that we have seen the kindness and generosity of God in the life and death of his own Son for us, how much more have we reason to give back a tenth! If those who understood only a little of God's blessing gave a tenth, surely it is a travesty to suggest that now that we understand so much more of God's great gift to us, we should give *less*. Quite the reverse! In the light of the great mercy and beneficence of Almighty God in giving his own life so that we may live, 10 per cent is an absolute minimum. The question we should ask is not, 'How much should I give?' but rather, 'In all good conscience, how much should I keep?'

Jesus commented on the poor widow who put two small pennies into the temple offering box (Luke 21:1–4). Materially, for the upkeep of the church, her offering was completely irrelevant. But in God's kingdom, it was a precious and priceless gift, way beyond any of the huge monetary gifts of the rich or titled. Why? Because it was a sacrificial offering. So if giving 10 per cent is not sacrificial for us, we need to give more until our giving *is* sacrificial.

For us as Christian, should not 10 per cent of our income go directly and without question back to God? If failing to give the tithe is to rob God, then it seems that our giving starts only after the 10 per cent has gone to God. As someone once said to me, 'It's not the 10 per cent God is primarily interested in—it's the 90 per cent.' If giving 10 per cent is not sacrificial, then we're not giving enough; perhaps we need to give 20, 50, or 90 per cent or more.

The jubilee system

Back in Leviticus, God instructed his people on how they were to live. These instructions included that God's people were to work the ground for six years and then have a year of rest in the seventh year, trusting God to provide for them even though they had not ploughed and planted and tended crops. They were simply to obey and trust that God would provide for their needs through the seventh year and on through the eighth year, until the crops were harvested.

Further, every fiftieth year (the 'jubilee year') they were also to leave the land fallow and not work the soil or plant crops. Again, this system was designed to teach God's people to trust *him* for their provision, rather than trusting their own resources. That meant that the year prior to a jubilee year had no ploughing or planting (year 49, one of the seventh years), and then the following year, *again* they were to do no ploughing or planting.

The purpose of the whole system was to remind God's people regularly and practically to trust in him alone for all their needs.

However, the people of God *never* implemented this jubilee system in all of their years from its inception to the return from the exile. They had never trusted in God's provision as they were meant to do.

Perhaps, then, the background to Malachi's words here is simply that they had not kept God's instruction and depended upon him. God through Malachi is urging them, 'Give as you are meant to give. Give sacrificially. Implement the jubilee system as originally intended, rather than relying on your own wealth. And if you do that, see if I will not provide as I always promised to do.'

Overall, the Old Testament assumption was that everything we have belongs to God. Stuart writes, 'The Old Testament perspective on wealth is that the best and first of it never has belonged to its temporary human controller ("owner"), but always has belonged to God. The first-fruits of one's labours, the firstborn of one's flocks, the best quality of one's possessions are God's innate property.'[3]

John Laing was a Christian who understood how money should work in God's kingdom. He worked tirelessly to build up his construction firm into a multi-million-pound business. Early on, though, he and his wife decided what they needed to live on, and lived off the same inflation-adjusted figure each year until his death. At one point in his life, fellow board members were astonished to discover the Laings were saving up to buy a new sofa. Despite the fact that he had earned millions of pounds through his life, when he died his possessions were worth £371. He had given away everything else he had earned. That challenges me.

Notice in all this that tithing—or rather, sacrificial giving—is required because it is intimately connected with worship. It is a deep expression of our gratitude towards and love for Jesus. One good way to consider the extent to which we love God is to measure it by our giving.

Testing God (3:10–11)

Malachi 3:10 provides a huge incentive to tithe: God wants his people to test him! There is a seeming conundrum here. The verse reads, 'And thereby put me to the test, says the LORD of hosts', but Deuteronomy 6:16 reads: 'You shall not put the LORD your God to the test.' Which is correct? Surely the Bible is not contradictory, is it?

The answer lies in the nature of the testing in each case. In Deuteronomy 6:16, the test concerns those who do not trust in God. They are 'testing' him by following false gods. This is how Jesus used the verse at his temptation. When Satan tempted Jesus to throw himself off the temple since the angels would catch him, Jesus quoted this verse, responding, 'It is said, "You shall not put the Lord your God to the test"' (Luke 4:12). If I put God to the test in this way, then I am submitting to the will of the devil, not the will of my Father. I am not trusting in God; I am trusting in Satan. The question for Jesus was not about whether the angels would catch him if he jumped off the top of the temple; it was whether to trust the devil or trust God. There is no greater false god than the devil! Do not test God in this way.

But in Malachi 3:10, the test is not about following false gods and trusting in them, but about trusting God and seeing him fulfil his promises. It means living his way, giving sacrificially, trusting in him— and seeing what happens (God will bless me, Mal. 3). This is the heart of Psalm 34:8: 'Taste and see that the LORD is good!' This is not a demand for the Lord to prove his existence to a sceptical world, but rather an invitation to his own people to trust in him and experience his faithfulness.

In Malachi 3:10–11, opening 'the windows of heaven' undoubtedly refers to rain. The climate in the Middle East is hot and dry for seven months of the year and rainy for the other five months. Rain was essential. Without rain, the crops could not grow, and that meant starvation. This was one of the reasons why the Israelites kept reverting to the worship of Baal: they believed that he was the god who enabled them to produce children and the land to produce crops. This is also why a prophecy of God's great blessing on the people was couched in agricultural terms: when it's time to plant, you'll still be harvesting the previous crop. As a result, throughout the Bible, rain usually signifies God's blessing. When the rains come, the crops grow and flourish, and provide food and income for the people. Deuteronomy 11:13–14 reminds us of the blessing of rain.

As noted earlier, the Hebrew here literally says 'unto a failure of sufficiency'. In other words, as long as God's sufficiency endures, his blessing will come. Since God is always and will always be sufficient, it means 'in perpetuity'. So, if you live in constant obedience, you can expect continual blessing. Verse 11 continues this agricultural blessing, with promises that the crops will be bountiful. Crop bounty is often a way of signifying God's favour, more often symbolic than literal (see Amos 9:13–15).

Conclusion (3:12)

As we said at the outset, this text is not only about our finances. Certainly the message is that if the people return to God by giving sacrificially, he will return to them: Christians must stop defrauding the Lord's house. We are to become God's wholehearted and abundantly open-handed people, so that the cloud may soon rise over our land and the heavens grow dark with rain.

But giving goes deeper than our financial giving. Malachi's underlying point is that salvation is found through repentance and faith—the giving of ourselves back to God. If we return—repent—God will bring salvation to us. The direct outcome of our salvation should be worship: giving to God the glory, honour and praise that are rightfully his. All of life is about giving. We give ourselves to God in trust, and we give to God our worship, honour and praise. This includes our finances but is much broader and deeper than that. Our finances reflect the inner and deeper realities of life. The gospel is a gift of God to us; our lives should reflect that giving heart.

The concept of 'gift' at the heart of life will have this result: 'Then all nations will call you blessed, for you will be a land of delight, says the

LORD of hosts' (3:12). Malachi's focus is once again upon all the nations, not just Israel or God's people. God's purpose in blessing his people as a result of their obedience is that other nations will see and call them blessed; that the nations will recognize a different way of life, leading them also towards repentance and faith.

The message of Malachi 3:6–12 is simple: life is about gift. Jesus epitomized this approach: 'For God so loved the world that he *gave*.' Our supreme Creator God *gave* his only Son. The supreme Sustainer of everything *gave* his life. So, if we are Christians, the call for us is to give. First, we are to give our lives to the Lord; salvation is found in no one else. Second, we are to give what we have (time, talents, finances, etc.) to the Lord. Third, we are to give our worship to the Lord. And the result? God, who desires to return to us and to send the rain from heaven, will gather in his people from all nations, and lead us inexorably to our eternal home with him—the final gift towards which we head.

Notes

1 The two words are *sub* (used here, with root meaning 'turn' or 'return') and *naham* (used in Job 42:6, for example, meaning to be sorrowful for wrong and to change one's mind).
2 Douglas Stuart, in Thomas E. McComiskey, *The Minor Prophets: An Exegetical and Expository Commentary* (Grand Rapids, MI: Baker Academic, 2018 [1998]), pp. 1369–1370.
3 Ibid., p. 1300.

Justification or judgement? The coming of God (3:13–4:6)

I remember once visiting a restaurant in Glasgow. As we ordered our food, we noticed some remarkable desserts at the counter. Sitting majestically in the chiller were a dark layered chocolate cake that was a good six inches tall, a huge strawberry and raspberry pavlova with a diameter of perhaps fifteen inches, and a giant twelve-inch chocolate cream-filled eclair. Back in our home town, friends of ours were helping with a production of *Les Misérables* and had constructed a beautiful four-tier wedding cake, and it, too, made your mouth water to look at it.

But the proof of the pudding is in the eating. The desserts in the chiller looked amazing and tasted equally wonderful (at least, I imagine so; we weren't able to try them all!). The wedding cake, on the other hand, was made of polystyrene covered in Polyfilla. It looked great, but was completely inedible. Whilst both looked wonderful, the desserts were destined to be heartily enjoyed by the customers in the restaurant, but the wedding cake was destined for the garbage.

In this last section of Malachi, we discover two destinies for the visible people of God. There are many in the church who look like they fear the Lord: they walk the walk and talk the talk. But not all of them are true followers of Jesus on the inside. Followers of Jesus have a very different destiny from those who are not his.

We noted previously that there is a common structure to the disputations in Malachi. This structure is that (a) God states something, (b) his people challenge his statement, and then (c) God expands on his statement and describes the judgement that will come unless things change. This sixth and final disputation follows the same pattern. It is introduced by an accusation from God: 'Your words have been hard against me, says the LORD' (3:13). The people respond with a protest: 'How have we spoken against you?' Then the disputation that follows falls into three parts: a contrast, a conclusion and a comfort.

A contrast (3:13–4:3)

This final part of Malachi concerns a clear contrast between those who fear the Lord and those who do not. An accusation is made by those who do not fear the Lord (3:13–15). Then from 3:16, 'those who feared the Lord' respond. Malachi draws our attention to both types of people and to their eventual destinies. He gives great encouragement to those who love God: vindication is coming. But there is a deep challenge for those who do not love God: judgement is coming.

Just as the Old Testament began in darkness and chaos (Gen. 1:1–2) but with the promise of life right around the corner (Gen. 1:3ff.), so here the prophet brings a note of darkness and destruction (Mal. 4:1–3), but with the promise of life right around the corner (4:4–6).

We must remember that this prophecy from God through Malachi is not directed to the world at large. It is not 'Destruction is coming to the pagan nations, but salvation is coming to the Israelites.' It is not about people *outside* the walls of the church. Rather, this prophecy concerns the covenant people of God: it is directed to those *inside* the church. The message is, 'Here, within the visible church, there are those who belong to the Lord and there are those who do not. There are believers and unbelievers in the church of God.' Some are destined for joy and contentment; others are destined for judgement.

The same is true today. There are many people who have been regular and committed churchgoers perhaps for years or even decades, but who are not, in fact, submitted to Jesus and therefore are not part of his kingdom people. Here, Malachi urges even the most hardened moralist to come to Jesus for forgiveness and restoration. 'Search your hearts,'

Malachi cries, 'and make sure you are part of God's invisible church. Be part of the true people of God who are saved, redeemed, forgiven and found.'

This contrast between those who serve God and those who do not—between those who are righteous (i.e. who live right) and those who are wicked (i.e. who live in rebellion)—is found particularly in 3:18 and 4:1. Those who do evil and who set themselves up over others and over God (the arrogant) will be set on fire, but those who live in submission to the Lord will be joyful.

Malachi highlights three facets of this contrast: discussion, designation and destination.

Discussion

Consider the way Malachi 3:14 is written: 'It is vain to serve God. What is the profit of our keeping his charge or of walking as in mourning before the LORD of hosts?' These people are saying that frequent repentance ('walking as in mourning') brought no benefits at all. Malachi's words here represent a discussion that God's people were having amongst themselves. They were asking, 'What did we gain from obeying God? What did you get out of it? I didn't get anything out of it either. And those who are against God prosper. We gained nothing by trying to be faithful. There is nothing to be gained by following God.'

Think about that for a moment. Amongst other things, corporate worship is meant to include speaking (or singing) truth to one another, urging one another on towards God. But here there is a complete reversal of that. Here, the people have come together to speak to one another lies about God and to urge one another away from the kingdom! They have come together not because they love the Lord and one another, but to encourage one another to be faithless and rebellious.

In Malachi 3:16, by contrast, those who *do* fear the Lord are talking with one another. What do they discuss? We don't know in detail, but the implication from this verse is that they discussed how to fear God and how to honour his name. In other words, they encouraged one another to be faithful, honouring God, repenting before him and submitting to him. 'Let us consider how to stir up one another to love and good works,' writes the author to the Hebrews (Heb. 10:24), and it seems that this is what they were doing.

In other words, in these verses a distinction is made in terms of their discussion. Those against God pull each other away from him, whilst those with God encourage one another towards him.

Our words are so important. As we gather together on a Sunday, does the treasure of Jesus flow from our lips as we interact with each other before, during and after the service? Or is our conversation full of the things of this world, with little thought for the Lord in whose very name we have met? Do I attend church in order to love and build up my brothers and sisters in Christ, both during and outside of the service? For those who are natural introverts (I count myself in that category), we have to push ourselves to talk to people and interact. But push ourselves we must. It is part of the essence of church.

We don't get together to discuss politics, football, music, movies or the weather. Rather, our conversation as believing people together should naturally include the treasure of our souls. Of course, those other things may form part of our conversation, but they will not be our focus. Christians are urged to encourage one another in their faith and love for Jesus, especially when they meet together for corporate worship.

In Matthew, Jesus said simply, 'Out of the abundance of the heart the mouth speaks' (Matt. 12:34). The words we speak reflect what is going on in our hearts. Our conversations reflect our convictions. And for me, at least, this pulls me up short, convicting me again about the state of my heart.

In Psalm 51 David pleaded, 'Create in me a clean heart, O God, and renew a right spirit within me' (Ps. 51:10). When Ezekiel prophesied, many years after David and two hundred years before Malachi, he wrote that God would remove our hearts of stone and give us hearts of flesh (Ezek. 36:26). Christians, then, are those who have had a spiritual heart transplant, and this transplant is a vital operation that brings life. Without it, death is assured. If we are Christians, God is in the process of renewing our hearts, and what is going on inside is borne out by our conversations with one another.

So there are those who fear the Lord from the heart and there are those who do not; this is the contrast of discussion. But there is also contrast in terms of designation.

Designation

Back in 3:15 we have what is perhaps the highest insult to a holy God. The people are suggesting that God loves evil and punishes good; that he who is blindingly morally pure and holy is in fact calling evil good and good evil. But the boot is on the other foot. It is not *God* who calls evil good and good evil, but them. Sadly, we have the same problem in our day.

To give just one example, the Bible is clear that all of life is given by God as a gift, all humankind is made in his image, and he has purposes for us right from the womb. And the Bible is clear that murder is wrong. But our society denigrates the weak and powerless. It argues that women should be free to kill their unborn children, and calls such freedom a good thing (although it may not be called 'good' by those aborted babies, if they had a voice). We know that the Holocaust was a bad thing, with 6 million Jews killed by those who called evil good. The recent film *Denial*[1] made this point exactly. But somehow in our modern twenty-first-century world, 42 million unborn babies—185,000 of them in the UK—are legally killed every year, and society declares this 'good'. And who stands up for the unborn? Who defends the weak and the fatherless?

Father, forgive us, for we know not what we do. It is not God who calls evil good and good evil; the boot is on the other foot.

These grumblers, these evil-doers, in 3:13–15 put God to the test and seem to escape his judgement. This is a negative testing. It is coming against God's law repeatedly and testing him to see whether or not he will do anything about it. The Hebrews grumble because they think such people escape. 'You do nothing about it,' they say to God.

But there are two problems with this. First, the people to whom Malachi writes continually fail to realize that God is not speaking to people outside the fold, but rather he is speaking to them. It is *they* who do not fear the Lord; it is *they* who designate God as unholy and unjust. *That* is the travesty. And the people who make the accusation are the very ones who are themselves unholy and unjust. Second, of course, the evil-doers (as they see them) who put God to the test will *not* escape his judgement: judgement will come eventually.

So what is the contrast in designation? It is simply this: unholy people designate God as unjust, but God designates holy people (that is, those who fear the Lord) as his 'treasured possession' (3:17). The word translated 'treasured possession' literally means 'personal property'. It is first used in Exodus 19: 'Now therefore, if you will indeed obey my voice and keep my covenant, you shall be my treasured possession among all peoples, for all the earth is mine' (Exod. 19:5). In other words, whilst it is true that God owns all things, there is a special way in which he owns his people. This may be why the translators have opted for 'treasured possession' rather than 'personal property'; it is a term describing God's particular and special ownership. If we are believers in Jesus, we are owned by him not just because he created us, but more deeply because he loves us and has chosen us. It is a heart ownership, as well as a legal ownership.

In one of my favourite television shows people transform dark, dank and dilapidated property into beautiful homes. Sometimes a property developer already owns ten or twenty houses. Suppose that when one such property developer finds another house she likes and buys it at auction, instead of developing it and selling it on, she chooses to develop it and live in it, and to make it her home. Now she owns this house more deeply—from the heart, you could say. She will build memories in it and have joy associated with it. Out of all the houses she owns, this one will truly be *hers*, the one she owns in a special way, with love and commitment.

God owns all things because he created all things. He is the legal and rightful holder of the title deeds. But if we are Christians, God lives within us by his Holy Spirit. He owns us now, not just because he is our Creator, but from his heart because we're his children. Love and commitment are involved. It is a deeper ownership, an ownership reflecting his amazing love which stooped to save.

There is further encouragement in 3:16: those who fear the Lord are written in his book of remembrance. But why does God need a book of remembrance? Is he likely to forget? Is it that, with the infinite number of things he has to remember day by day, he can't hold it all in and is worried he might forget?

No. This book of remembrance is, perhaps, like the annals that a king might have kept regarding people and what they had done during their time in the kingdom. God, as King, keeps perfect records. These are records that stand as a lasting testimony that his people are his. To be written in the book of remembrance is a great comfort. God's true people are on the wedding-guest list for the marriage supper of the Lamb of Revelation 19. Betrothal has occurred. Now we live waiting expectantly for that final day.

If we have submitted to Jesus in repentance and trust, our names also are written in God's book of remembrance. We will be saved on that final day. Things may be hard for us now. We may face all kinds of difficulties. Perhaps we see evil prosper and the wicked prevail. But we *will* be saved. 'They shall be mine, says the LORD of hosts' (3:17). The 'LORD of hosts' is

Adonai Sabbaoth, meaning 'Lord of the armies'. He is powerful beyond all of creation combined. And if you are a Christian, you are his, and only by overcoming his power could you change that—something no one can possibly come close to achieving. The stronger-than-the-universe God states emphatically, 'You are mine.' What a blessing! And what an encouragement!

So we have noted a contrast in discussion and a contrast in designation. But, as with the difference between the desserts and the wedding cake, there is also a contrast in destination.

Destination

Malachi prophesies loud and clear about the Day of the Lord. Judgement will come, he says, a judgement that is burning bright. For some, it will be a furnace that burns them up (4:1). They will be like stubble, and set on fire.

But for others, it will be like the noonday sun (4:2). For them, righteousness—all that is right, good, wholesome and holy—will rise like the sun. The darkness will be dispelled. Everything will be brought to light. Those who have been maligned will be vindicated. The truth will out. Wrongs will be righted. Shaky faith will be cemented. Formerly quavering lips will now give full-bodied praise. Healing will come. And they will be filled with joy. No longer will evil-doers prosper. No longer will the wicked escape. Wickedness and evil will be trampled underfoot. The imagery used in this verse is of a battle won, of triumph in war.

This is a stark contrast in destination. Perhaps Jesus had this very text in mind in Luke 10 when he spoke to the seventy-two after they returned from mission: 'I have given you authority to tread on serpents and scorpions, and over all the power of the enemy, nothing shall hurt you. Nevertheless, do not rejoice in this, that the spirits are subject to you, but rejoice that your names are written in heaven' (Luke 10:19–20). See the connection that Jesus makes: they trample evil underfoot *because* their names are written in heaven. I think this is a reference back to the book of remembrance.

Some farmers keep their cows indoors during the winter, both to keep them safe (especially the pregnant ones) and to feed them up ready for the spring. When those cows are brought out of the barns and set free in the fields in March or April, even the older cows jump around like newborn calves at the joy of their new-found freedom (there are videos of this online)! As Christians, we have been born again and we're now in the period of being 'fattened'—kept inside for the winter, if you like. We are being prepared, made ready for that great day. On *that* day, we will be released and, like the cows, we will exult in the freedom that comes after a time of confinement and waiting for deliverance (4:2). Vindication will finally come.

Malachi finishes his prophecy with a conclusion and a comfort.

A conclusion (4:4–6)

To conclude, Malachi says, in essence, 'In the light of all this, consider three people: Moses, Elijah and the Lord.' So we will do exactly that.

Moses

First, Malachi urges that the people look back at the law: 'Remember the law of my servant Moses' (4:4). This is a reference not just to the Ten Commandments but to the whole of the Law of Moses. That is, he is urging us to consider the first five books of the Bible—Genesis through to Deuteronomy, or the Pentateuch, as it is called. Malachi is not simply asking the people to bring the words of the law to mind; he has a far more active idea.

When one of my children comes into the house and dumps a school bag on the lounge floor, I might say, 'Remember what we said about school bags?' I'm not asking for them to say, 'Oh yes, I remember', as if all I require is cognitive remembrance. No, when I say, 'Remember . . . ', I'm actually giving an imperative: 'Pick up the bag and put it where it belongs!' It is a call to obedience.

In a similar manner, Malachi is calling people to obedience. The Law of Moses not only speaks of God's holiness, it also demands *our* holiness. And that demand for holiness, as has been the intention throughout Malachi, is meant to lead us towards repentance. The idea is: 'Look at Moses and see your sinfulness, failure and wickedness. Then turn back to God for forgiveness and seek salvation from him.'

Elijah

Malachi then tells them to look forward to the coming Elijah (4:5).

If we look at the abortion travesty across our country and our world, we might say we need a William Wilberforce to come and generate change. By saying that, we would not mean we need Wilberforce himself to rise from the grave and come back; we would mean that we need someone with his tenacity, conviction, diligence, determination and eloquence to come and demonstrate God's truth to a world lost in a fog.

It is similar here. Who is this Elijah about whom Malachi speaks? It is not the Elijah of 1 and 2 Kings, the one who did not die but was taken up to heaven in a whirlwind (2 Kings 2:11). That Old Testament Elijah was not going to return literally to continue his ministry. No, the Elijah of whom Malachi speaks is a new Elijah—someone with Elijah's tenacity and faith.

When John the Baptist was asked, 'Are you Elijah?' he responded rightly and emphatically, 'No!' (John 1:21). Elijah was in heaven; John was not him! However, Jesus said, 'For all the Prophets and the Law prophesied until John, and if you are willing to accept it, he is Elijah who is to come' (Matt. 11:13–14). Jesus is saying that John the Baptist *is* Elijah! The picture seems contradictory at first. Which is right?

Of course, there is no contradiction here. John the Baptist was not literally the Old Testament Elijah come back from heaven (which was

John the Baptist's point in John 1:21), but he *was* the one coming in the spirit and power of Elijah. Later, Jesus said, '"Elijah has already come, and they did not recognize him . . . " Then the disciples understood that he was speaking to them of John the Baptist' (Matt. 17:12). Jesus called John the 'Elijah who is to come'. An Elijah was needed to inaugurate the last days, and John the Baptist was this figure. He was the one who came in the spirit and power of Elijah, the one who would point the way to the Messiah. This new Elijah had a vital job: to introduce Jesus.

This brings us to the third person Malachi points us towards.

Jesus

Malachi has just brought together Moses and Elijah. This is important because Moses and Elijah represent the whole of redemption history up to the time of Jesus. The message of the Old Testament is, 'God is holy, you are sinful; you can't help yourself—you need saving.' But underneath that message is the fact that the Old Testament is God's word about Jesus. In Luke 24, two disciples were travelling on the road to Emmaus when Jesus met them. Then, 'beginning with Moses and all the Prophets, he interpreted to them in all the Scriptures the things concerning himself' (Luke 24:27). The Old Testament in its entirety is described as 'Moses and all the Prophets'. So Moses and Elijah together stand for all the Hebrew Scriptures. Jesus was making the point that the whole of the Old Testament points to him as the one who can put us right.

Therefore, it should be no surprise to us that at Jesus' transfiguration (Matt. 17; Mark 9; Luke 9), the two people with whom he meets on the mountain are Moses and Elijah. The whole of the Old Testament is being represented before the one who fulfils it all.

Moses saw the fire of God in the burning bush, in the pillar of fire and as it burned upon Mount Sinai in glory and holiness. Elijah saw God's fire as it fell on the sacrifice at Carmel and burned it up, as it raged at the mouth of the cave as he cowered there, and in the chariots and horses as he was taken up into heaven in a whirlwind. They knew something of the fire of God.

But at the transfiguration, up another mountain, alongside Moses and Elijah, the prophet *like* Moses, and the one greater than Elijah—Jesus himself—stands. These two men are not surrounded now by the shining fire of heaven they have experienced before, but by the shining of Jesus' glorious righteousness. Jesus is transfigured before the disciples, too, shining bright as the noonday sun. What a wonderful foretaste of Jesus' second coming, when his eternal glory will be seen once more! At the transfiguration, the Son of Righteousness himself had come.

Of course, at his first coming, Jesus came to die. He came to make salvation possible for his people. But one day he will return, to bring righteousness to his own people and judgement to everyone else. Malachi 4:6 is clear: God will bring reconciliation between himself and his children. 'He will turn the hearts of fathers to their children and the hearts of children to their fathers, lest I come and strike the land with a decree of utter destruction.'

It is clear that the purpose of this whole prophecy is to bring people to repentance so that they will find themselves in eternal day rather than under a curse. The term translated 'decree of utter destruction' is *herem*—a curse, a decree of destruction as things are devoted utterly to the Lord. God is saying quite simply that if people will not devote themselves to him, then one day he will devote all things to himself. The burning fire of his holy judgement will come. Anything against him will be set ablaze and face destruction.

This final verse uses the word 'turn' which we saw back in 3:7, meaning 'turn' or 'repent'. Jesus will turn fathers back to their children and children back to their fathers. He will turn his children back to their Father. This is the heart of repentance: turning away from sin and back to God. Ultimately, this is a work Jesus does, not a work we do ourselves. Jesus works in the heart—that is the central image in Malachi 4:6.

So there are two options: either Jesus turns someone's heart, or God strikes them with destruction. Either someone is devoted to God because of the work of Jesus in their heart to turn them back to their Father, or they remain in their rebellion and face destruction.

Having looked at the contrast and the conclusion, we finally come to comfort.

A comfort

All this talk of 'Are you in or out?' reminds me of the referendum in 2016 in which the UK voted to leave the European Union—to be 'out'. But the purpose of the text in Malachi—indeed, of the whole prophecy—is that we would be 'in'. God speaks through Malachi in order to bring us to repentance if we are currently 'out', and to lead us further in if we are 'in'. It is not designed to engender doubt about our salvation if we're Christians.

In fact, in this text we have blessed assurance: due to the work of Jesus at the cross we can be certain of our future. We recognize our sinfulness, our rebellious hearts. We know we deserve nothing less than condemnation before Almighty God. We know that the fire of judgement is coming and that we cannot save ourselves. But we can throw ourselves upon the mercy of Jesus who took upon himself the judgement and wrath we deserve. We can ask him for forgiveness, and we can ask him to be our Lord and our King from this time forward. If we do so, a scroll of remembrance is written. Our names are engraved on his hands.

This is the difference between Job and Job's wife. Job's wife is known for only one thing: she said very simply, 'Curse God and die' (Job 2:9). By contrast, Job struggled, questioned and wondered. Faintly and falteringly he trusted, though he was not sure and he did not understand the reasons for his situation. He had no notion of the heavenly battle taking place out of sight. But right at the end of the book, after God has finally spoken (although still without giving Job any answers!), God says to the friends of Job, 'You have not spoken of me what is right, as my servant Job has' (42:7). And God said of Job, 'Consider my servant Job!' He was proud of him, if I may put it that way. Faltering, failing, broken, weak, questioning, wondering—yet God was pleased with him.

Countless Christians struggle on day by day with long-term sickness, pain, addictions or repeated sin. We feel that we fall more than we rise; that we fail more often than we succeed (this is certainly true of my own experience). But it is inspiring to see Christians who struggle on as Job did. They keep going. That is a beautiful, challenging thing. It shines with the light of Jesus. From a human perspective, I have no idea how such people keep going. It would seem that the easiest thing in the world would be to 'curse God and die'. But they don't do that; they press on.

Thus, their names are engraved on his hands. Their eternity is secure. Their Lord is supreme. Their life is hidden with Christ in God. And he is 'proud' of them. If we are Christians, God is 'proud' of us also. Perhaps we think that while that may apply to other people, 'it doesn't apply to me'. But Malachi is clear: if I have repented and believed, it applies to me also.

We must not look back at all these words from God written in Malachi and say, 'I cannot live up to that; I am unable, inadequate. God must be so disappointed in me. Perhaps even my eternity is in doubt.' Rather, we should look at all these words from God through Malachi and say, 'I cannot live up to that; I am unable, inadequate—but thanks be to God, for he *is* able. He loves me as his own. And he is delighted in me!' Know this for sure: your citizenship is in heaven, bought for you by the precious blood of Jesus, and there is no turning back. He is Lord, and he loves you. Your destiny is sure and certain.

If you have never turned away from your sin and knelt at the feet of Jesus, do it now. Cry out to him. Ask him to forgive you and to save you. Jesus is coming back—and that will result in either vindication for him and judgement upon yourself, or vindication for you and judgement upon him. His desire is for your heart, soul, mind and strength. You cannot earn it. You cannot buy it. But you can submit and enjoy it—that love relationship with your Creator who loves you beyond anything you can ever know.

On that final day, we will all face either justification or judgement. It is our true nature that matters: are we truly part of the people of God, or are we faking it? Like the cakes in the chiller cabinet and the wedding cake, our destiny is either joy or being put out with the rubbish. Either we will be enjoyed by Jesus and enjoy our eternity with him, or we will be judged and condemned. The central question for us is therefore simple: God is coming—are we ready?

Note

1 This 2016 film is based on Deborah Lipstadt's book *History on Trial: My Day in Court with a Holocaust Denier*, a book about how Lipstadt, a Holocaust scholar, was sued by Daniel Irving, who denied the Holocaust ever happened.